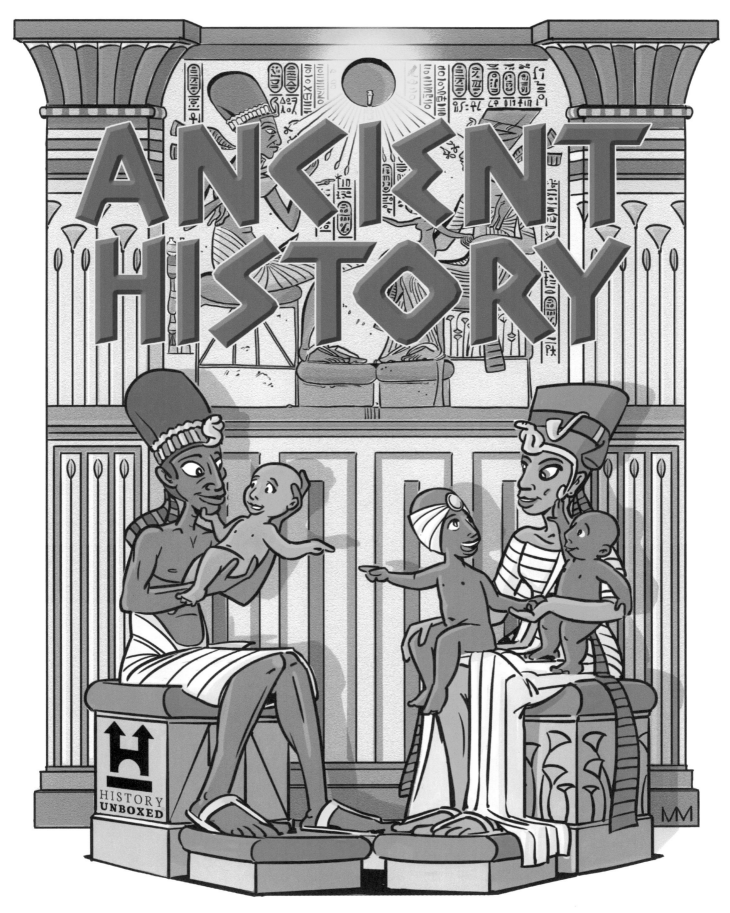

ANCIENT HISTORY

A SECULAR EXPLORATION OF THE WORLD VOLUME 1

STEPHANIE HANSON AND ELIZABETH HAURIS

ANCIENT HISTORY
Copyright © 2021 by History Unboxed

Contents

Photo by Phumzile Phala

How Humans Spread Across the Earth

Imagine yourself standing on the east coast of Africa, looking out at the sea. The waves crash against the shore, and you can't take your eyes off of the horizon. You wonder if there is anything else out there. Turning away from the ocean, you look at the land stretching away from you in all directions. How far does it go? Are there other people you haven't met? When our species, *Homo sapiens sapiens*, evolved around 150,000 years ago, they all lived in East Africa. Other species like the Neanderthals had already spread out to Europe, and eventually, we started traveling the world too. We don't know the exact routes, but historians have a general idea.

The journey took thousands of years and many generations as modern humans meandered across the surface of the earth. As much as 85,000 years ago, people began to leave Africa. Some walked into Asia, while others sailed across the Red Sea. For the most part, they stuck to the coast with its abundant supply of food. The first travelers to leave Africa were the ancestors of everyone in the Middle East, everyone in Europe, everyone in Asia, and everyone in the Americas (DNA evidence is inconclusive about Australian Aboriginal ancestry). Millenia passed and the people continued to wander on foot and by sea. We don't know exactly when they reached Australia. It could have been a hundred thousand years ago or only forty thousand years ago. As they crossed Europe, they encountered Neanderthals. Did they compete for resources? Did they fight or have children together? All we know is that after about 15,000 years of contact, the Neanderthal had gone and *Homo sapiens* remained. By 45,000 years ago, they had settled across Europe. The journey wasn't over yet. Other groups continued up the east coast of Asia and took advantage of the Ice Age climate. The lower sea level meant that a land bridge called Beringia connected Asia and North America. All those nomadic groups had to do in order to cross the Pacific Ocean was walk. The ancestors of Indigenous Americans slowly traveled across North America between thirty and thirteen thousand years ago, making their way down the continent and into South America by about fourteen thousand years ago.

What were our ancestors like? They had fire. They had language by about 50,000 years ago. They lived in small hunter-gatherer groups and observed rituals for significant events such as the death of a loved one. They discovered agriculture about 10,000 years ago and then things really began to change.

1

A Note From Our Historian

Growing up, I would not have said that history was my favorite subject. Yet, many of my favorite school memories revolve around history. In fourth grade, I asked my teacher for permission to put on a play about the American Revolution, and she said yes. In sixth grade, we put on a Greek festival for the school and I played the Oracle at Delphi. In middle school, my teacher regaled us with gory tales from Upton Sinclair's *The Jungle*. My freshman history teacher introduced me to world religions. I opted for independent study for history my senior year, and learned that I loved researching history. But when I got to college, I did not even consider history as a major. I thought it had to be all about dates and battles and names. Then, in a required American history course, my professor had us read *Devil in the White City* by Erik Larsen, and I learned that history had narratives beyond dry facts. I couldn't stop reading about the manhunt for a truly terrible serial killer amidst the magic of a World's Fair. I switched my major to history and sat enthralled while my Caribbean history professor told us stories, such as one about Anne Bonney, a terrifying female pirate. The good professors all told stories. The dry ones showed slides with names and dates. Invariably, my grades reflected the teaching style of the professor.

I eventually became an elementary school teacher. I asked my students to write down their favorite memories during the year and put them in a jar. One of their favorite projects was when teams of students created civilizations, simulated archaeological digs, and put on a museum of their discoveries. It set the field for an interest in history in a way that an objective written on the board could never inspire.

History Unboxed is all about inspiring a lifelong love of history and teaching children that history is, first and foremost, about people. Sometimes they shock us, sometimes we see ourselves in the people who lived so long ago. Everyone has gaps in their historical knowledge. It's impossible to learn about every civilization and every important person in tens of thousands of years in human history. Instead, we hope that our young historians will develop curiosity about the past. Some historical events continue to have an impact on our world today. Others are simply fascinating in their own right. We want to whet your appetite so that you and your learners will continue to seek out stories of long ago.

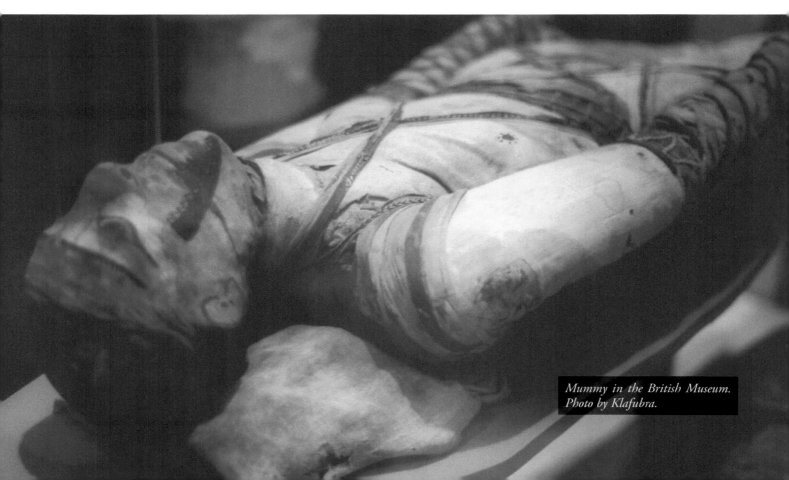

Mummy in the British Museum.
Photo by Klafubra.

The Parthenon, a temple dedicated to Athena, located on the Acropolis in Athens

On Ancient History

Generally, prehistory is defined as all of history before the invention of writing. That's a bit complicated as writing developed at different times in different areas. But the general definition of the ancient history time period begins with the invention of writing in Sumeria and Egypt, around 3200 BC/BCE. But how do we define the end of the ancient period? Typically, western scholars use the fall of Rome in 476 AD/CE as an arbitrary end point. While that is a very Eurocentric date, we have chosen to use it as a general guideline. However, you will see that certain civilizations bridge multiple eras and do not fit neatly into categories. We have attempted to give a broad overview of ancient history worldwide. There are so many cultures we would

have loved to include, like the Celts or Polynesians. We have settled for choosing a few from a traditional history course of study and a few that are rarely, if ever, covered in ancient history classes. Your journey begins with a Stone Age culture and takes you through the ancient history period to a civilization straddling the transition between the Ancient period and the Middle Ages. We have taken a secular approach that acknowledges the role of religion in history without favoring any single religion as the truth.

Educator's Note:

This book takes a secular approach to the discussion of one religion, meaning that no religion is presented as truth. Some religions described in this book are still practiced today. If you are a religious family, we recommend pre-reading any chapters that discuss your faith tradition.

The Continent Of Australia, Home To The Tribes Of

ADNYAMATHANHA
ALAWA
ALYAWARRE
AMANGU
BAADA
BAKANAMBIA
BALARDONG

GAARI
GADJALIVIA

NAKAKO
NAKARA
NANA
OITBI
OLA
OLKOLO
PAKADJI
PANDJIMA
PANGERANG
PANGKALA

JAARA
JABURARA
GAMBALANG JADIRA
DAII GEAWEGAL KAANTJU
DAINGGATI GIA KABALBARA
DALABON IDINDJI KABIKABI
DALLA ILBA KADJERONG MAIAWALI
EORA ILDAWONGGA LAIA MAIJABI
ERAWIRUNG JAADWA LAIRMAIRRENER MAIKUDUNU
EWAMIN JAAKO LAMALAMA MAIKULAN
MAITHAKARI

RAKKAIA
RAMINDJERI
SPINIFEX PEOPLE
TAGALAG
TAGOMAN
TARGARI
UALARAI
UALAYAI
UMPILA
& MANY MORE

A note about tenses: For the sake of consistency, we have used the past tense throughout this text. However, because the Australian Aboriginal culture is a living culture, much of what you will read is still true today.

The Australian Aboriginals are the oldest continuous civilization on Earth. These Aboriginals arrived in Australia via a land bridge, now underwater, between 40,000 and 50,000 years ago. Over the years, they formed clans that spoke different languages but still shared certain cultural characteristics. Prior to European arrival, all Australian Aboriginals were nomadic hunter-gatherers who revered nature and had a strong oral storytelling tradition. Women gathered seeds, roots, berries, and insects, while the men hunted animals and fish. Depending on the region, men hunted with either boomerangs (southeastern Australia) or spear throwers, or fished with nets and bone-barbed spears. Given the harsh conditions of most of the continent of Australia, insects formed an important part of the Aboriginal diet. They were an important source of protein, and in the case of honeypot ants, also a source of sweetness. They also ate kangaroo, the tail being a particular delicacy, snakes, emu, and other birds. They lived in clans that intermarried, and had overlapping

ABORIGINAL AUSTRALIA

territories with shared dialects. The Aboriginals also had common religious traditions.

Aboriginal religious beliefs centered around a concept that has been translated as "Dreamtime," but this is an incomplete translation. The Anangu spoke a language called Pitjantjatjara, and used the word "Tjukurpa." Tjukurpa included stories of the creation time and long ago history, in which Australia was an empty land that was then shaped by the activities of distant ancestors. It also included rules for behavior, communities, and ceremonies, even dictating who can marry and what and how to eat. There was also a strong idea of stewardship of the land, with an emphasis on knowledge of animals and plants. Many of the stories were kept secret. People learned more over time as they were initiated into higher and higher levels of knowledge. Many of the stories and ceremonies are still kept secret today. We do know that the ceremonies used instruments like the bullroarer, which can be heard over great distances, and the didgeridoo. Both were played only by men, for rituals such as initiations. Only certain initiated men could play the bullroarer, and outsiders were forbidden from participation in those ceremonies. The didgeridoo is a slightly newer instrument, only about three thousand years old, and used primarily in Northern Australia. Women may have used an instrument called "clapsticks" to accompany the didgeridoo. Clapsticks are similar to rhythm sticks, and are clapped together to beat out rhythms. Because the Aboriginals have no written language, beliefs and knowledge were passed down through music, dance, and art.

Australian artwork provides some of the earliest archaeological evidence of humans in Australia, with some cave paintings dating back to around 40,000 years ago. These paintings of animals, people, and trees were painted with ochre, a reddish pigment, and charcoal. Later, Aboriginals used dot paintings in sand or on bark to tell stories, with each dot representing a person, object, or animal.

Aboriginals still live in Australia today, making up a little over one percent of the population. Prior to European arrival in the early 17th century, around half a million people lived in Australia and spoke over 250 different languages. Because of English settlement practices and subsequent laws, today only about thirty Aboriginal languages have survived. Australian Aboriginals only gained full citizenship in the 1960s, and even today debate continues about the rights of Aboriginals to their sacred lands. Some have lifestyles similar to those of their ancestors, while others have moved to cities and become assimilated into white Australian culture. No matter where they live, Aboriginals continue to gather at corroborees, gatherings where actors sing, dance and tell sacred stories, while musicians play the didgeridoo and participants paint their bodies with ochre.

Five thousand years ago was when the dingo, Australia's wild dog breed, appeared in Australia for the first time. At the time, it was likely a domesticated animal used for guarding or hunting, but they became wild over the next several thousand years. We know that Aboriginal culture changed over time as stone tools were refined and settlement expanded across the continent, but without a written record, we know little about changes that took place between the introduction of the dingo and the arrival of Europeans thousands of years later.

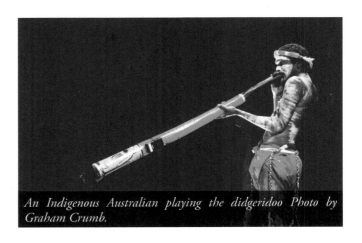

An Indigenous Australian playing the didgeridoo Photo by Graham Crumb.

The Creation Story

Once upon a time, nothing lived upon the surface of the earth. Underneath, however, a Rainbow Serpent, the Great Mother Snake, slept deeply for many years. When she finally awoke and slithered out into the open, all that she saw was flat, empty, and dry. "This won't do," she said to herself, and used her magic to make rain. The rain continued without stopping for days, weeks, months, and years. The Rainbow Serpent's body left deep tracks in the dirt that filled with water, creating rivers and waterholes. When she pushed her nose into the earth, the soil piled up into hills and mountains. And in other places, milk from her breasts soaked the Earth, making it fertile for grasses and forests and flowers to grow.

Finally, the Rainbow Serpent felt satisfied with her work and slithered back into the Earth to wake up the other creatures sleeping there. The first to wake were the land animals: the dingoes, the kangaroos, and the tree-frogs. The dingoes did not need much water, and so she led them to the desert. The bush made a perfect home for the grass-loving kangaroos, and the tree-frogs followed the Rainbow Serpent to the rainforest where it was cool, dark, and wet.

Next to awaken were the birds. The eagles flew high and far to the mountains, while the emus, who couldn't fly, followed the Great Serpent to the plains where they could run and run as much as they liked.

The barramundi, the fish, followed her to the rivers; the frogs to the ponds; and the turtles to the lagoons. More and more animals awakened, and the Rainbow Serpent led them to the perfect home. Ants, beetles, spiders, and scorpions all found their homes under rocks, in crevices, and in the sand.

Last of all, the Rainbow Serpent brought a woman and a man out of the darkness under the earth, and to a place with plenty of food and water. She taught them how to respect all living creatures—the creatures who were their cousins. She showed them the rocks and trees and waterholes, telling them that these places were sacred parts of the world she had created. And she taught them how to live on the land that she had created, warning them that they were only guardians of this land. If they did not care for the land properly, if they abused the land, then she would re-emerge and make the world again, this time without woman or man.

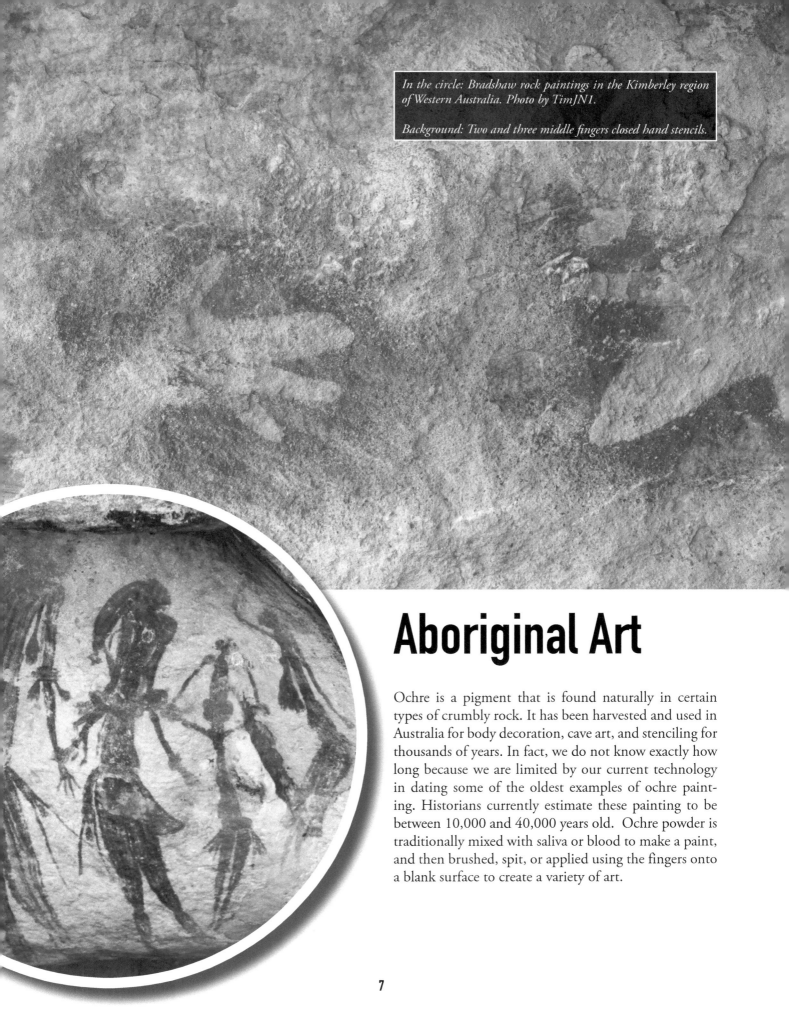

In the circle: Bradshaw rock paintings in the Kimberley region of Western Australia. Photo by TimJN1.

Background: Two and three middle fingers closed hand stencils.

Aboriginal Art

Ochre is a pigment that is found naturally in certain types of crumbly rock. It has been harvested and used in Australia for body decoration, cave art, and stenciling for thousands of years. In fact, we do not know exactly how long because we are limited by our current technology in dating some of the oldest examples of ochre painting. Historians currently estimate these painting to be between 10,000 and 40,000 years old. Ochre powder is traditionally mixed with saliva or blood to make a paint, and then brushed, spit, or applied using the fingers onto a blank surface to create a variety of art.

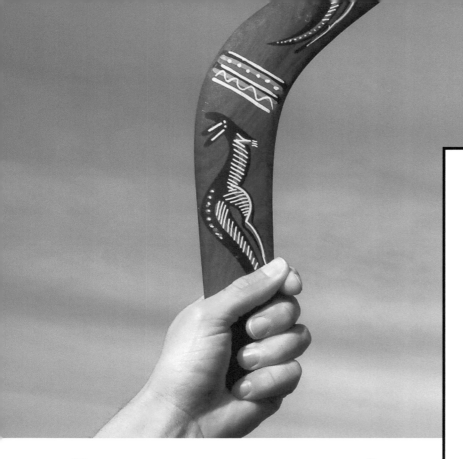

Boomerangs and Hunting

Although throwing sticks for hunting existed throughout the ancient world, the name we use for them today comes from Australia: boomerang. Boomerang comes from the language of the Turuwal tribe of Australian Aboriginals. The oldest Aboriginal boomerangs are around 10,000 years old, while others have been found that are as much as 30,000 years old. In more recent history, the Egyptian boy-king Tutankhamen had a collection of boomerangs. Although we use the word boomerang to describe something that bounces back or returns to the thrower, those used for hunting were actually designed to fly straight and not return. The returning boomerang may have come about accidentally when hunters were actually trying to fine-tune their hunting sticks to get them to fly straight. The boomerangs used in hunting were large, and were used either to flush birds into nets or to knock down larger prey such as kangaroos or emus. When aimed carefully, the boomerang hit with enough force to break the neck of an emu on impact. They were also used in hand to hand combat. The Australians even clapped two boomerangs together as musical instruments. Who knew a simple piece of wood could be so versatile?

FURTHER READING

All Ages
Dreamtime: Aboriginal Stories by Oodgeroo. While this book is out of print, it is well worth finding a used copy. Written by an Aboriginal activist and poet, the stories are accompanied by dot paintings in a contemporary Aboriginal style done by an Aboriginal artist. This book weaves together traditional tales with memories of the author's upbringing in modern Australia.

Ages 5-9
Down Under (Vanishing Cultures Series) by Jan Reynolds. The author follows a young girl on her walkabout. The photographs and story are about a modern family, but everything in the book is part of traditional Aboriginal culture. It helps to make the connection between ancient history and modern people, while providing a vivid picture of how Australia's original inhabitants have lived for thousands of years.

Ages 10-15
Uluru: Australia's Aboriginal Heart by Caroline Arnold. Arnold provides information about one of the most famous places in Australia, connecting geology, ecology, and anthropology in this book about the formation formerly known as Ayers Rock. The book is out of print, but is widely available used and in Kindle format.

Ant Candy and Witchetty Grubs

If you think eating insects sounds gross, you are in agreement with many modern westerners. But *entomophagy*, or eating insects, is an age-old and global tradition. In Australia, Aboriginal women gathered insects along with plant foods to supplement the diet in between hunting trips led by the men. Because sources of natural sugar were rare, many Aborigines ate honeypot ants as a source of sugar. These ants store a sweet nectar in their abdomen, expanding a special sac until it is as the size of a small grape. Other insects served as valuable sources of protein. Today, many Aboriginal Australians still eat insects at least sometimes even though they eat modern foods too.

Aborigines used to eat thousands of species of plants and animals. These included large animals like kangaroos and emus, lizards, shellfish, fish, grubs, wild berries, bananas, apples, yams, figs, and many kinds of seeds and bulbs. They ate eggs, including platypus eggs. Aborigines learned how to process and cook foods that were toxic if eaten fresh and raw. Food was baked in earth ovens or roasted on coals. Very little food was wasted. They ate all parts of animals, including muscle, fat, and organs. It was a healthy, nutrient dense diet. They did not have many food-related illnesses. Sometimes food was scarce, but the Aborigines were able to make homes in places that Europeans later considered unlivable.

Today, poverty rates are high among indigenous Australians. Many worry about having enough to eat. There are not many food markets in distant settlements, so it's hard to find fresh fruit and vegetables. They are often expensive. People end up eating a lot of flour, sugar, and processed foods. Food related diseases are common. Some people are turning back to traditional foods when they cannot buy enough food, and others are turning back to traditional foods to be healthier. The Aborigines of today eat about 40 different plant and animal species. They still hunt kangaroos and cook them traditionally. Witchetty grubs remain a delicacy. Some traditional foods, called "bush food" or "bush tucker" have even shown up in fancy restaurants. Even kangaroo is common at Australian grocery stores. Most commercial bush food businesses are owned by white Australians because of the country's legacy of colonialism, but there is a movement working towards more indigenous owned businesses.

Honeypot ants compared to a human hand. The dark dorsal sclerites are widely separated by the stretched arthrodial membrane of the inflated abdomen of each replete. Photo by avilasal.

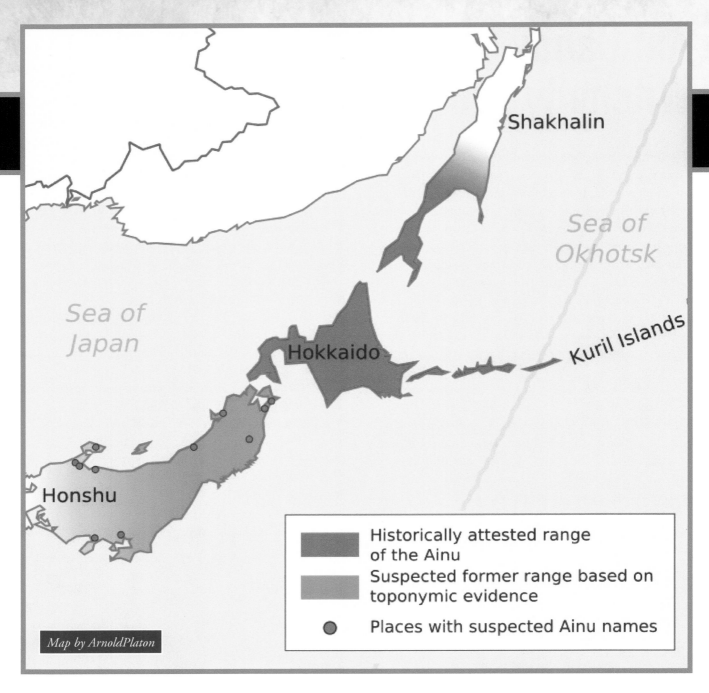

Map by ArnoldPlaton

Legend:
- Historically attested range of the Ainu
- Suspected former range based on toponymic evidence
- ⬤ Places with suspected Ainu names

Shakhalin

Sea of Okhotsk

Kuril Islands

Sea of Japan

Hokkaido

Honshu

The Jomon people lived in Japan around 5,000 BC/BCE . This is so far in the past that it is considered "pre-historic" meaning that it was before written records; before the beginning of what most historians consider "history." This time is also called The Stone Age since stone was the material that was widely used to make tools. The Jomon are possible ancestors of the indigenous Ainu people of Japan, while the Yayoi people, who arrived in Japan around 2,000 years ago, are the most likely ancestors of modern Japanese citizens. The Jomon period of Japan lasted from 13,680 BC/BCE to 410 BC/BCE, from the Mesolithic period to the Ancient period.

During the Early Jomon Period, the Jomon people created extremely specialized stone tools and a trade in these tools, ceramics, and other craft goods stretched across the entire archipelago of Japan and possibly to Korea on the mainland. They also began developing more permanent settlements.

Throughout history, hunter-gatherer cultures like the Jomon have led nomadic lives, following the food from place to place. The Jomon were unusual hunter-gatherers in that they lived relatively stationary lives. They did have seasonal homes, but these pit houses were permanent structures clustered together in

THE JOMON

small villages. They tended to use the villages as a sort of base camp, with teams traveling for a few days in order to forage, hunt, or fish instead of relocating frequently. They may also have cultivated a small number of plants, collected from the wild. The Jomon were among the first people to domesticate dogs, using them for hunting. In the winter, the Jomon hunted deer and wild boar when the more easily collected plants and shellfish were scarce. They used pit traps and nets to catch large game, with the dogs driving the animals towards the traps. They honored hunters and held special ceremonies at the end of the hunting season. They were also unusual as a hunter-gatherer culture because of their high level of craft production, including clay cooking vessels and clay figurines. They may have produced some of the world's earliest pottery.

The Jomon left behind an incredible number of artifacts, particularly those made of clay and stone.

The wealth of archaeological information means that we know more about the Jomon than about most other Neolithic cultures. In other parts of the world we know that the wheel was invented simultaneously in several cultures around 4500 BC/BCE: in Mesopotamia, in the northern Caucasus Mountains, and in central Europe, but we don't know who was first! Some cultures were also exploring proto-writing: pictograms used to communicate. Because there are no written records anywhere in the world, historians must use archaeological evidence and other scientific methods, such as DNA analysis, to draw hypotheses about what these cultures were like. This means that historians often disagree about each other's conclusions. Unless we invent a time machine, it's likely that we will never have solid answers about the prehistoric period.

Face of a large earthen figure (estimateur original height one metre). Late Jomon, c. 1500BCE. Shidanai Iwateken. Owned by Bunkacho (Agency of Culture), Tokyo.. Photo by PHGCOM.

A jar with spirals. Final Jomon, Kamegaoka style. Photo by PHGCOM.

The Sophisticated Stone Age

When we hear the words "Stone Age," it usually conjures up some images in our minds: people living in caves, dressing in animal skins, and using lumpy stone tools. It's amazing to learn that the Jomon didn't live this way at all! They built villages where hundreds of houses sheltered people who came together to trade tools, clothing, and store food. These villages were sometimes connected by roads that the Jomon built. They domesticated and trained dogs for hunting. They gathered nuts, shellfish, and plants from the surrounding areas and crafted beautiful clay pots for cooking, food storage, and religious rituals. Their stone and wood hunting weapons were so effective that they were able to hunt tuna, whales, sharks, bear, and boar. In fact, modern hunting tools have failed to outperform the harpoons that the Jomon invented and used. They wove fabric, tanned leather, made baskets, and created stone and clay art. They even had a way to manage sewage in their villages that was much cleaner and healthier than many other systems that were used much later in history: they dug pit toilets and layered them with shells. The calcium in the shells neutralized the waste, preventing it from rotting and polluting the area. Even the dogs were trained to use these pit toilets! The lifestyle of the Jomon shows us a level of comfort and sophistication that people don't usually associate with this time in prehistory. So, when you think of the Stone Age, remember the Jomon and all of their amazing accomplishments.

FURTHER READING

The Jomon people are not often studied in Western schools, so there are no children's books about the Jomon as far as we know. Many of the available books for adults about the Jomon are printed in Japanese. However, the author of the following website has spent ten years researching Japanese history, and there is an incredible amount of information about Jomon Japan, including some unusual ideas, like what we can learn from studying ear wax. Use the links at the right to navigate across different topics.

https://heritageofjapan.wordpress.com/just-what-was-so-amazing-about-jomon-japan

A Brief History of the Baskets of the World

Do you have any baskets in your home? Then you are part of a tradition dating back thousands of years. Basketmaking is one of the oldest crafts, dating back as far as 26,000 years ago, and possibly longer. It may even be the oldest craft in the world, an ancestor of other ancient crafts. Early people originally used limbs, leaves, and vines woven together to create vessels that would have been vital in a hunter-gatherer society. These baskets could be used to collect and store fruits, nuts, seeds, and dried meat. They could also be backpacks, baby carriers, cradles, storage containers, or fishing nets. The techniques used to twist and weave the fibers together into a basket may have inspired the development of weaving fibers into fabric. And it's possible that the first clay pots may actually have been basket liners used in cooking. When a fire got too hot and burned away the basket fibers, it would fire the clay and leave a waterproof vessel.

Thinking of baskets as an ancestor to pottery makes sense when you look at early Jomon pottery. The Jomon pottery mimics the fibers of a basket, sometimes with fibers pressed into the clay to leave a pattern behind. These baskets give us our name for these people, as the word Jomon means "cord markings" in Japanese. The Jomon began making baskets around 10,000 BC/BCE, and they were largely utilitarian. Different regions had baskets for rice cultivation, grain harvest, or fishing. They were also used in food storage. One archaeological discovery included baskets of acorns in a food storage pit.

The twisted cords that formed the structure of the baskets were made of bamboo, strips of bark or wood, and wild vines. While the purpose may have been utilitarian, the baskets were also sometimes decorative in appearance. One surviving basket from the Jomon was made of tree bark, decorated with a cloud pattern, and then lacquered. Even today, thousands of years later, it is a vivid orange color. It also had a lid, made of bent and woven bark. These ancient baskets began a long-standing tradition of Japanese basket-making that has continued into the modern day. Their hexagonal weave pattern spread throughout Asia and then into the rest of the world through trade.

Wicker baskets. Photo by AugustineChang.

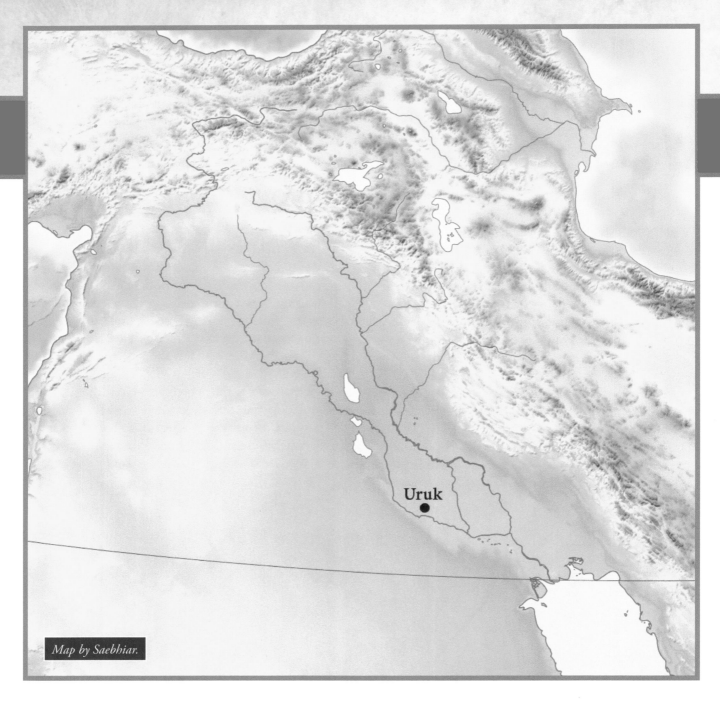

Map by Saebhiar.

The Epic of Gilgamesh, a mythical story about the historical king, is widely considered to be the world's first great work of literature. Although his life is largely known through myth, archaeologists believe they have discovered his tomb, and he is widely accepted to be an historical figure as well as a mythical one.

The city of Uruk lasted thousands of years, from 4500 BC/BCE to 3000 BC/CE. Located in the southern region of Sumer, in modern-day Warka, Iraq, the city had many names. The Aramaic word was Erech, and Uruk may be the same city of Erech mentioned in the Bible. Uruk was the first true city of the world,

with tens of thousands of inhabitants. This first city was truly a city of firsts: the first writing, the first architectural work on stone, the first ziggurat, the first cylinder seal (and symbol of personal identity), and the first large-scale, freestanding sculpture. The first writing was cuneiform, wedge-like symbols pressed into clay using a stylus. The first examples were pictographs, or symbols, but over time, cuneiform became more symbolic than pictorial, and finally, after 2600 BC/BCE, became phonetic. In addition to the Epic of Gilgamesh, the people of Uruk recorded temple rituals, government lists, and religious texts, such as the Hymn to Inanna.

URUK

Everything before a written record is considered pre-history, so Uruk exists at the very beginning of human written history. The city of Uruk remained the largest and most powerful city until around 3000 BC/BCE. Ultimately, the city was unable to maintain control over its other territories and conflict with Babylon further reduced the city's prominence.

In the city, freed from the labors of agriculture, inhabitants turned to other professions. The power in the city rested with the king, priests, and other members of the ruling class. But stone cutters, gardeners, weavers, smiths, cooks, jewelers, and potters all had their place in the city as well. The weavers wove linen cloth for the upper class and wool cloth for everyone else (linen is a very labor-intensive fiber to produce from flax, while wool threads are simply spun from wool that has been washed and combed). The city would have been a colorful place, with painted statues, dyed fabrics, and black, red and white cone mosaics. These mosaics were made of cones of clay stacked upon each other and stuck into plaster, pointy end first. They decorated both temples and palaces in Uruk. Religion played a major role for the people of Uruk, who believed that the rise of their city was the work of the gods, and particularly the goddess Inanna. Inanna had her own district within the city, separate from the older district dedicated to her grandfather, Anu. One of the artifacts discovered in Uruk is the marble Mask of Warka, one of the earliest known realistic depictions of the human face. Archaeologists believe that this mask was intended to represent Inanna, and was probably from one of the temples in her district. It likely once belonged to a life-sized statue, with matching hands and feet made of marble and a wooden body.

What else was going on in the world while Gilgamesh ruled over Uruk? Although other civilizations existed at the same time, such as the Jomon civilization in Japan, written history had barely begun. Chinese legends have led historians to conclude that China's first emperor, the Yellow Emperor, ruled during this time. Like Gilgamesh, the Yellow Emperor is partially a figure of myth and partially an historical figure. In Egypt, the Old Kingdom was just beginning, with Egypt's first dynasty. Sumer wasn't the only area developing writing, as Egyptian hieroglyphs developed around the same time. Historians have been unable to determine whether writing evolved independently in Egypt or if the Egyptians were influenced by the Sumerians. However, writing also began in the Indus River Valley, just after the reign of Gilgamesh, in the cities of Harappa and Mohenjo-daro. Uruk may have been the first great city, but other cities quickly followed as human civilization spread across the middle East, northern Africa, and Asia.

A general view of the Uruk archaeological site at Warka in Iraq. The site of Uruk was discovered in 1849 by William Kennett Loftus who led the first excavations from 1850 to 1854. Photo by SAC Andy Holmes (RAF).

The Epic of Gilgamesh

Gilgamesh was a king of Uruk, but the fantastic stories written about him go far beyond the life of any real man. The Epic of Gilgamesh depicts him as part god and the epitome of all things amazing and regal.

The epic was written on clay tablets in cuneiform and translated during the 19th century, giving us the story of Gilgamesh—sometimes a good king, sometimes not—and his adventures. Gilgamesh's driving motive in the epic is to find a way to avoid death. In the end, he seeks immortality through building. In a way, Gilgamesh did achieve immortality through the epic itself. There have been many translations and retellings of The Epic; some directed at children and some that retain the original story's more adult themes.

The Epic of Gilgamesh is the earliest known great work of literature. We recommend two different retellings. For our 5-9 year olds, we recommend the *Gilgamesh Trilogy*, by Ludmilla Zeman. The first book, *Gilgamesh the King*, tells the story of Gilgamesh's friendship with Enkidu. For 10-15 year olds, we recommend the wonderfully illustrated *Gilgamesh the Hero* by Geraldine McCaughrean.

"The dream was marvelous but the terror was great; we
must treasure the dream whatever the terror"
--Anonymous, The Epic of Gilgamesh

"Gilgamesh is strong to perfection...
Gilgamesh is awesome to perfection.
Who can compare with him in kingliness?
Who can say like Gilgamesh: "I am King!"?
Whose name, from the day of his birth, was called
"Gilgamesh"?
Two-thirds of him is god, one-third of him is human.
The Great Goddess [Aruru] crafted the model for his
body, she prepared his form ...
... beautiful, handsomest of men ... perfect"
--Anonymous, The Epic of Gilgamesh

Possible representation of Gilgamesh as Master of Animals, grasping a lion in his left arm and snake in his right hand, in an Assyrian palace relief, from Dur-Sharrukin, now held in the Louvre. Photo by Jastrow.

Cuneiform

Cuneiform was the first kind of writing in the world. The invention and development of cuneiform is considered to be the most important contribution to come from the Sumerians and the city of Uruk. Cuneiform started out as a picture based writing: with one image to represent a king, another for a sheep, and so on; but later it developed into a phonetic writing where letters stand for sounds.

Cuneiform was written with a wedge shaped stick called a stylus that was used to make triangle marks in a clay tablet. The name "Cuneiform" came later (we do not know what the Sumerians would have called their writing) and contains the Latin word "cuneus" meaning "wedge shaped." Since clay tablets can last for thousands of years under the right conditions we have many artifacts containing Sumerian cuneiform. Language experts have been able to translate these tablets giving us wonderful stories from ancient times, like The Epic of Gilgamesh and The Descent of Inanna. What an amazing treasure from the past: stories that people wrote and told more than 4,000 years ago!

Tablet V of the Epic of Gilgamesh The Sulaymaniyah Museum, Iraq. Photo by Osama Shukir Muhammed Amin FRCP(Glasg)

Art in Ancient Uruk

Uruk, the first city, was a thriving center for art. Mesopotamian art had certain characteristics that made it stand out. The cone mosaics and sculptures were new and revolutionary forms of art. The walls were painted with frescoes in orange, black, and red. The artwork depicted people at work or on battlefields, as well as both realistic and fantastical animals. While artists had already tried making their work realistic, Mesopotamian artists were among the first to develop a specific style. The people in artwork often had larger than life eyes. Beards and hair were depicted through elaborately swirled carvings. Even carvings depicting clothing had rich texture simulating woven cloth.

Cone mosaics were used to decorate the walls and pillars of important buildings. Thousand of cones made of clay (about the size and shape of an ice cream cone, but with no hole for ice cream) were painted white, black, or red and pressed, pointed end first, into a wall. The colored flat ends formed beautiful geometric patterns: triangles, diamonds, and zigzags.

The cylinder seals recovered from Uruk are the oldest in the world. Seals were used in ancient times as a signature: the pattern on the seal could be pressed into a clay tablet leaving a person's unique mark. But they stand for more than just a name.

The seals of Uruk are the first example historians have found of the value of the reputation of individuals in a community. Each seal was designed to say something about the person it belonged to, and, using the seal, a person could be recognized as a unique individual. Those doing business could have a written record of a person's previous dealings and know the value of his word.

FURTHER READING

All Ages
Lugalbanda: The Boy Who Got Caught Up in a War by Kathy Henderson. Lugalbanda was likely Gilgamesh's father and this beautiful story is based on two poems written on cuneiform even before the oldest version of the epic of Gilgamesh. The introduction and afterword provide information about the culture, while the story itself gives a peek into the world of Uruk.

Ages 5-9
Gilgamesh the King by Ludmila Zeman. This is the first in the Gilgamesh trilogy series, a picture book series that makes the Epic of Gilgamesh accessible for our youngest learners. The illustrations are wonderful and the storytelling is engaging. If you enjoy the first book, the sequels are *The Revenge of Ishtar* and *The Last Quest of Gilgamesh.*

Ages 10-15
DK Eyewitness Books: Mesopotamia by Philip Steele. This book covers all of the civilizations in the area, with beautiful illustrations of artifacts from the period. Like all of the Eyewitness books, the illustrations are fantastic for all ages, but the reading level is best for ages ten and up.

Life in Ancient Mesopotamia (Peoples of the Ancient World) by Shilpa Mehta-Jones. This is a great source for daily life, geography, religion, and more with great illustrations and photographs of artifacts.

The Epic of Gilgamesh translated by Andrew George. This translation is poetic, readable, and written by a scholar of Sumerian history. It is the top recommended translation. Best for those on the upper end of this age group because of mature themes. You can share sections of the poem for younger readers.

Ancient fast food containers?

In modern-day internet speak, BRB means Be Right Back. But if you are an archaeologist studying Mesopotamia, BRB stands for Bevel Rimmed Bowls. BRBs are so common that many archaeologists and historians just use the abbreviation. In garbage pits, sometimes half the pottery turns out to be BRBs. So far, thousands have been discovered. So what are they?

They are small, molded bowls made of a mix of clay and chaff (discarded grain shells). They have a beveled, or sloped, edge. On the outside, they are rough. Inside, they are smooth, still showing the imprint of the wet fingers that smoothed the clay. The rim was likely trimmed with a blade. Fired at a low temperature, they are porous. That means any liquid is likely to be soaked up by the clay. How small? They are about four inches tall, seven inches wide at the mouth, and a little over three inches wide at the base. They hold about six cups, but the bowls are not completely regular in size.

These bowls can tell us a little bit about Uruk culture, but we have to make some guesses. Here are some discussion questions to get you started:

Did these objects belong to wealthy or upper class people only?
Probably not. They were not well-made (in fact archaeologists often call them ugly), they were mass-produced, and there were far better-made pottery vessels.

How were they made?
We don't know fur sure, but here is one possible method: the maker dug hollows in the ground, mixed together wet clay and chaff, and dropped a lump of clay into the hollow. Then they punched a hole into the middle and covered the whole thing with straw. The straw was lit on fire, and when it burned away, the clay was hardened. We know that the bowls were fired at lower temperatures, and the bowls have been reproduced with this method.

What did they hold?
Archaeologists don't agree. They may have been used as a measure for laborer's daily rations; as bowls to hold religious offerings; for serving food at large banquets hosted by the aristocracy; making yogurt (least likely because they are porous); or as molds for baking bread. The first and last hypotheses are the most popular. We are fairly certain they weren't used for liquid.

Why were they thrown away?
Because they were mass produced and not very well made, they have been compared to plastic food takeout containers, or plastic bags. Some people might have reused them, but most of the time, they were intended for single use.

How do we know the bowls were important?
The pictogram for "eat" was the human head plus the bowl shape. Later on, the symbol for bread looked like a BRB. And they made a lot---over ¾ of all ceramics found in Uruk are BRBs.

Photo by Schauschgamuwa.

The Decent of Inanna
A Sumerian Myth

Edited for History Unboxed

Some imagery may be frightening. Educator preview is recommended to ensure content is appropriate for your students

Chapter 1

From the Great Above she opened her ear to the Great Below.
From the Great Above the goddess opened her ear to the Great Below.
From the Great Above Inanna opened her ear to the Great Below.

My Lady abandoned heaven and earth to descend to the underworld.
Inanna abandoned heaven and earth to descend to the underworld.
She abandoned her office of holy priestess to descend to the underworld.

She placed the shugurra, the crown of the steppe, on her head.
She arranged the dark locks of hair across her forehead.
She tied the small lapis beads around her neck,
Let the double strand of beads fall to her breast,
And wrapped the royal robe around her body.
She daubed her eyes with ointment called "Let him come, let him come,"
Bound the breastplate called "Come, man, come!" around her chest,
Slipped the gold ring over her wrist,
And took the lapis measuring rod and line in her hand.

Inanna set out for the underworld.
Ninshubur, her faithful servant, went with her.
Inanna spoke to her, saying:
"Ninshubur, my constant support,
My sukkal who gives me wise advice,
My warrior who fights by my side,
I am descending to the underworld.
If I do not return
Go to Nippur, to the temple of Enlil.
When you enter his holy shrine, cry out:

'O Father Enlil, do not let your daughter
Be put to death in the underworld.
Do not let your bright silver
Be covered with the dust of the underworld.
Do not let your precious lapis
Be broken into stone for the stoneworker.
Do not let your fragrant boxwood
Be cut into wood for the woodworker.
Do not let the holy priestess of heaven
Be put to death in the underworld.'

If Enlil will not help you
Go to Eridu, to the temple of Enki.
Weep before Father Enki.
Father Enki, the God of Wisdom, knows the food of life,
He knows the water of life;
He knows the secrets.
Surely he will not let me die."
When Inanna arrived at the outer gates of the underworld,
She knocked loudly.
She cried out in a fierce voice:
"Open, the door, gatekeeper!
"Open the door, Neti!"
I alone would enter!"

Neti, the chief gatekeeper of the kur, asked:
   "Who are you?"

She answered:
   "I am Inanna, Queen of Heaven,
   On my way to the East."

Neti said:
"If you are truly Inanna, Queen of Heaven,
On your way to the East,
Why has your heart led you on the road
From which no traveler returns?"

Inanna answered:
"Because . . . of my older sister, Ereshkigal,
Her husband, Gugalanna, the Bull of Heaven, has died.
I have come to witness the funeral rites.
Let the beer of his funeral rites be poured into the cup.
Let it be done.

Neti spoke:
    "Stay here, Inanna, I will speak to my queen.
    I will give her your message."

Neti, the chief gatekeeper of the kur,
Entered the palace of Ereshkigal, the Queen of the
Underworld, and said:
"My queen, a maid
As tall as heaven,
As wide as the earth,
As strong as the foundations of the city wall,
Waits outside the palace gates.

On her head she wears the the crown of the steppe.
Across her forehead her dark locks of hair are care-
fully arranged.
Around her neck she wears the small lapis beads.
At her breast she wears the double strand of beads.
Her body is wrapped with the royal robe.
Her eyes are daubed with the ointment called, 'Let him
come, let him come.'
Around her chest she wears the breastplate called
'Come, man, come!'
On her wrist she wears the gold ring.
In her hand she carries the lapis measuring rod and line."

When Ereshkigal heard this,
She slapped her thigh and bit her lip.
She took the matter into her heart and dwelt on it.
Then she spoke:
"Come, Neti, my chief gatekeeper of the kur,
Heed my words:
Bolt the seven gates of the underworld.
Then, one by one, open each gate a crack.
Let Inanna enter.
As she enters, remove her royal garments.
Let the holy priestess of heaven enter bowed low."

Neti heeded the words of his queen.
He bolted the seven gates of the underworld.
Then he opened the outer gate.
He said to the maid:
    "Come, Inanna, enter."

When she entered the first gate,
From her head, the crown of the steppe, was removed.

Inanna asked:
    "What is this?"

She was told:
    "Quiet, Inanna, the ways of the underworld
are perfect.
    They may not be questioned."

When she entered the second gate,
From her neck the small lapis beads were removed.

22

Inanna asked:
    "What is this?"

She was told:
    "Quiet, Inanna, the ways of the underworld are perfect. They may not be questioned."

When she entered the third gate,
From her breast the double strand of beads was removed.

Inanna asked:
    "What is this?"

She was told:
    "Quiet, Inanna, the ways of the underworld are perfect. They may not be questioned."

When she entered the fourth gate,
From her chest the breastplate called "Come, man, come!" was removed.

Inanna asked:
    "What is this?"

She was told:
        "Quiet, Inanna, the ways of the underworld are perfect.
    They may not be questioned."

When she entered the fifth gate,
From her wrist the gold ring was removed.

Inanna asked:
    "What is this?"

She was told:
        "Quiet, Inanna, the ways of the underworld are perfect.
    They may not be questioned."
When she entered the sixth gate,
From her hand the lapis measuring rod and line was removed.

Inanna asked:
    "What is this?"

She was told:
    "Quiet, Inanna, the ways of the underworld are perfect. They may not be questioned."

When she entered the seventh gate,
From her body the royal robe was removed.
Inanna asked:
    "What is this?"

She was told:
        "Quiet, Inanna, the ways of the underworld are perfect.
    They may not be questioned."

Naked and bowed low, Inanna entered the throne room.
Ereshkigal rose from her throne.
Inanna started toward the throne.
The Annuna, the judges of the underworld, surrounded her.
They passed judgment against her.

Then Ereshkigal fastened on Inanna the eye of death.
She spoke against her the word of wrath.
She uttered against her the cry of guilt.

She struck her.
Inanna was turned into a corpse,
A piece of rotting meat,
And was hung from a hook on the wall.

Chapter 2

When, after three days and three nights, Inanna had not returned,
Ninshubur   dressed herself in a single garment like a beggar.
Alone, she set out for Nippur and the temple of Enlil.

When she entered the holy shrine,
She cried out:
"O Father Enlil, do not let your daughter
Be put to death in the underworld.
Do not let your bright silver
Be covered with the dust of the underworld.
Do not let your precious lapis
Be broken into stone for the stoneworker.
Do not let your fragrant boxwood
Be cut into wood for the woodworker.
Do not let the holy priestess of heaven
Be put to death in the underworld.'

Father Enlil answered angrily:
"My daughter craved the Great Above.
Inanna craved the Great Below.
She who goes to the Dark City stays there."

Father Enlil would not help.

Ninshubur cried out:
"Oh Father Enki, do not let your daughter

Be put to death in the underworld.
Do not let your bright silver
Be covered with the dust of the underworld.
Do not let your precious lapis
Be broken into stone for the stoneworker.
Do not let your fragrant boxwood
Be cut into wood for the woodworker.
Do not let the holy priestess of heaven
Be put to death in the underworld.

Father Enki said:
"What has happened?
What has my daughter done?
Inanna! Queen of All the Lands! Holy Priestess of Heaven!
What has happened?
I am troubled. I am grieved."

From under his fingernail Father Enki brought forth dirt.
He fashioned the dirt into a kurgarra, a creature neither male nor female.
From under the fingernail of his other hand he brought forth dirt.
He fashioned the dirt into a galatur, a creature neither male nor female.
He gave the food of life to the kurgarra.
He gave the water of life to the galatur.
Enki spoke to the kurgarra and galatur, saying:
"Go to the underworld,

Enter the door like flies.
Ereshkigal, the Queen of the Underworld, is moaning
When she cries, 'Oh! Oh! My inside!'
Cry also, 'Oh! Oh! Your inside!'
When she cries, 'Oh! Oh! My outside!'
Cry also, 'Oh! Oh! Your outside!'
The queen will be pleased.
She will offer you a gift.
Ask her only for the corpse that hangs from the hook on the wall.
One of you will sprinkle the food of life on it.
The other will sprinkle the water of life.
Inanna will arise."

Chapter 3

The kurgarra and the galatur heeded Enki's words.
They set out for the underworld.
Like flies, they slipped through the cracks of the gates.
They entered the throne room of the Queen of the Underworld.

Ereshkigal was moaning:
    "Oh! Oh! My inside!"

They moaned:
    "Oh! Oh! Your inside!"

She moaned:
    "Ohhhh! Oh! My outside!"

They moaned:
    "Ohhhh! Oh! Your outside!"

She groaned:
    "Oh! Oh! My belly!"

They groaned:
    "Oh! Oh! Your belly!"

She groaned:
    "Oh! Ohhhh! My back!"

They groaned:
    "Oh! Ohhhh! Your back!"

She sighed:
    "Ah! Ah! My heart!"

They sighed:
    "Ah! Ah! Your heart!"

She sighed:
    "Ah! Ahhhh! My liver!"

They sighed:
    "Ah! Ahhhh! Your liver!"

Ereshkigal stopped.
She looked at them.
She asked:

"Who are you,
Moaning - groaning - sighing with me?
If you are gods, I will bless you.
If you are mortals, I will give you a gift.
I will give you the water-gift, the river in its fullness."

The kurgarra and galatur answered:
    "We do not wish it."

Ereshkigal said:
    "I will give you the grain-gift, the fields in harvest."

The kurgarra and galatur said:
    "We do not wish it."

Ereshkigal said:
    "Speak then! What do you wish?"

They answered:
    "We wish only the corpse that hangs from the hook on the wall."

Ereshkigal said:
    "The corpse belongs to Inanna."

They said:
"Whether it belongs to our queen,
Whether it belongs to our king,
That is what we wish."

The corpse was given to them.

The kurgarra sprinkled the food of life on the corpse.
The galatur sprinkled the water of life on the corpse.
Inanna arose. . . .

Map by US Federal Central Intelligence Agency (CIA)

Mohenjo-daro, or Moenjodaro, is largely unknown because, unlike famous sites like the Pyramids in Egypt or Damascus in Syria, it was only rediscovered in 1922 by R. D. Banerji, an officer of the Archaeological Survey of India. Located in what is now Pakistan, the site has only been partially excavated and has been listed as a UNESCO World Heritage Site by the United Nations in 1980.

The city was made of unbaked clay stones and laid out according to strict rules, denoting an early system of city planning. Along those lines was the early use of irrigation and water management, i.e. an ancient sewer system, which is a necessary feature for any large urban center. The center of the city had a great stupa mound which housed the Great Bath, Great Granary, the College Square, and many other public and private buildings. The rest of the city was arrayed around the great mound in a strictly planned design.

Mohenjo-daro, which literally means "mound of the dead" in the modern Sindhi language, was the largest city in the Harappan Civilization, also known as the Indus Valley Civilization. They existed from roughly

INDUS VALLEY

3000 BC/BCE until somewhere around 1700 BC/BCE when most of their city-sites had been abandoned. Scholars believe that this was most likely due to drought and a loss of trade with Egypt and Mesopotamia. They spread through what is now Pakistan, northern India, and all the way to the Iranian border. They were a center of trade and learning in the region for centuries. They developed their own standardized system of weights and measurements, their own writing system, detailed ceramics and beads, and metallurgy techniques using bronze, copper, tin, and lead. They created ceramic seals of unicorns and elephants as well as terracotta and bronze figurines of people and animals. They even had their own religion, though we know little about it today. Some Hindu scholars have looked for connections to their own religion, such as the Harappan's practice of cremating the dead. However, a lack of information and evidence keeps them from making a definite connection.

What is often overlooked in Mohenjo-daro, and in most civilizations and history, is their use of games. Dice and game pieces have been excavated from the ruins, and while we cannot know the rules, we do know now that play and games are a vital part of culture and human development. Many of the great cultures also had games that were their own, and the Indus Valley is no exception. We believe that some the games at Mohenjo-daro were played on a cloth or dirt board and resembled Chutes-and-Ladders. What we recognize now as chess originated in India around the 6th century AD/CE, with similar versions in China. Go originated in China in the 5th century BC/BCE, versions of Backgammon and Checkers were played by the ancient Romans, the Egyptians played games of dice and a popular board game called Senet which dates back at least to 2686 BC/BCE and was discovered on hieroglyphics in the tomb of Hesy-Ra.

The "dancing girl of Mohenjo-daro"

Henna

Henna is a plant that grows wild in northern Africa and the eastern Mediterranean region. It has been used for thousands of years as a dye for hair, skin, and textiles, as well as for its therapeutic benefits. The plant originated in Africa, but the seeds spread to the Mediterranean coast through the droppings of migratory birds. While the plant grew over a wide area, the ancient Egyptians may have been the first to cultivate henna. Around 4000 BC/BCE, the Egyptians learned that they could use metallic salt mordants[1] with henna to dye cotton and wool red. During this time, Mohenjo-daro was using madder root and betel nut to make red dyes for fabric. But the Egyptians went beyond textiles and used henna to cover up gray hair. They also used it as a skin treatment, but not as body art. Henna use spread along with the plant, and by 3000 BC/BCE, the people of the Indus River Civilization had begun using henna to decorate both themselves and their livestock. It's possible that women used henna to dye their lips and palms just as the Sumerians were doing during this period. By 1550 BCE, the Libyans, the Tunisians, the Canaanites, and the Syrians were all using henna for body art, and the Egyptians had produced a papyrus all about the various beneficial uses of henna. They used henna to treat skin disorders such as fungal skin diseases. Henna is also mentioned in the Bible in the Song of Solomon as a plant called camphire.

Today, henna remains popular as a hair dye and ink for temporary tattoos. It has a deep ritual significance for many cultures originating in the Middle East, South Asia, and North Africa. Hindus, Muslims, and Jewish people all use henna as part of ceremonies such as marriage, religious festivals, and life cycle rituals. Henna has also become a popular form of body art for secular purposes all over the world.

1. Mordant: A substance used in the dyeing process to make the dye colorfast.

Henna applied on both hands.
Photo by AKS.9955

Unicorns

Modern depictions of unicorns usually feature a beautiful horse with a long flowing mane and a single shining horn. Next to a modern unicorn, the ancient Indian unicorn might seem a little homely, but it's actually quite fantastic. This unicorn, according to Greek and Roman sources, is the very first mythological unicorn. It must have played an important role for the people of Harappa and Mohenjo-daro, for unicorns are found on around seventy percent of all of the seals discovered by archaeologists in that part of the world. Archaeologists have also discovered single-horned figurines with a hole in the belly, which would allow the unicorn to be carried on a stick during religious ceremonies. Today, historians debate the identity of the animal that inspired the unicorn. It could be the nilgai antelope or an amalgamation of multiple animals such as an ox with an antelope horn. Other composite creatures are seen in the artifacts of both cities.

One of these creatures has the head of a man, the trunk of an elephant, and the body of a bull. A three-headed beast found on one seal has a unicorn body and one unicorn head, joined with two antelope heads. Another animal is reminiscent of Dr. Dolittle's pushmi-pullyu: it has a rhinocerus body and an antelope head on either end. A beast with the front end of a tiger and the rear end of a bull decorates one copper tablet. Although unicorns were the most important of these mythological creatures, all the evidence indicates that the Indus people had a rich mythology that was an integral part of their daily life.

Toys & Games

Play was an important part of life for the people of the Indus River civilization, both for children and for adults. The most popular toys were little terracotta and wooden carts that mimicked the full-size versions used by farmers and merchants. Some even had fabric tops to protect the contents from the sun, and were filled with miniature goods like tiny clay pots. While many of these little carts have been found, suggesting their popularity, archaeologists have not found any vehicles of war, like chariots. Perhaps it is because their civilization was primarily peaceful for most of its existence. These little carts, like their larger counterparts, were pulled by oxen. These oxen were also made of baked terracotta and clay, some of them with wobbly heads tied on with string. Archaeologists have also found clay figurines of cats, dogs, monkeys, and squirrels. Some of these toys originally had wheels and string attached so a child could drag the toy. Some of the figurines have pot bellies and holes in the base as well as holes for moveable arms. Some archaeologists think these were used as puppets. Other children played with toy boats, rattles, or bird whistles. They placed their "lovies" in terracotta beds and lovingly covered them with woven blankets. In other words, they had a lot in common with children today!

Food In The Indus Valley

Indus Valley pottery, 2500–1900 BCE. Photo by Daderot.

Archaeologists have known for a while about the basic diet of the people in the Indus civilization. They looked at human teeth, animal bones, and the preserved remains of food items. Other products, like ginger and cinnamon, grew locally but left no obvious archaeological evidence. Recently, scientists found a new technique to extract starch molecules from cooking surfaces, cow teeth, human teeth, and around fifty other sources. From there, they discovered what they call a "proto curry" of eggplant, turmeric, ginger, and salt. The people of Harappa and Mohenjo-daro enjoyed a varied diet, although it was likely simple in preparation. They raised cattle for beef, and possibly for milk that was made into cheese. Archaeologists found perforated pots that could have been used in cheesemaking. They also raised sheep, goats, and chickens. In addition, they had a rich hunting environment with wild game such as buffalo, fowl, deer, antelope, and wild boar. The river provided fish and shellfish. Fertile soil was perfect for growing a wide variety of fruits and vegetables, including dates, grapes, melons, figs, mango and okra. They also cultivated grains, such as wheat and millet. The majority of people actually ate a mostly plant-based diet, and overwhelmingly, the human remains indicate good dental health. They cooked over a hearth or in a brick fireplace, using clay vessels. In wealthy homes, they also had metal cooking vessels and serving dishes.

FURTHER READING

All Ages
Daily LIfe in the Indus Valley Civilization by Brian Williams. This book is rich with information and has fantastic little text boxes called "How Do We Know" about the evidence that gave historians information to draw their own conclusions.

Ages 5-9
Smart Green Civilizations: Indus Valley by Benita Sen. This book is part of a series connecting past and present through environmentalism. In this volume, learn about the clothing, cities, and activities of the people who lived in Mohenjo-Daro.

Ages 10-15
The Indus Valley (Excavating the Past) by Ilona Aronovsky. Aronosky is a historian who specializes in teaching children about this period of history. She presents the information in easily digestible snippets. She also has a time travel novel about the period, *The Indus Investigators*, which has limited availability but is a fun way to explore the era.

This is a photo of a monument in Pakistan. Design is based on the Indus Priest/King Statue. The statue is 17.5 cm high and carved from steatite a.k.a. soapstone. It was found in Mohenjo-daro in 1927. It is on display in the National Museum, Karachi, Pakistan. Photo by Soban.

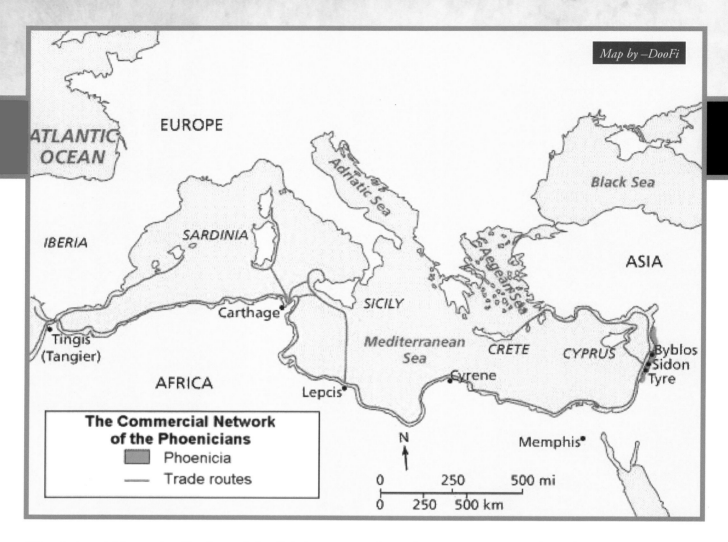

Map by —DooFi

EUROPE

ATLANTIC OCEAN

Black Sea

IBERIA

SARDINIA

Adriatic Sea

Aegean Sea

ASIA

Tingis (Tangier)

Carthage

SICILY

Mediterranean Sea

CRETE

CYPRUS

Byblos
Sidon
Tyre

AFRICA

Lepcis

Cyrene

Memphis

The Commercial Network of the Phoenicians

■ Phoenicia

— Trade routes

N

0   250   500 mi
0   250   500 km

Like their neighbors, the Greeks and the Babylonians, Phoenicians lived in city states, loosely allied in order to fight off outside invaders. A king ruled over this confederation, first from the city of Sidon, and then from the city of Tyre. You can still visit these cities today, in modern day Lebanon. At the time, the Phoenicians traded throughout the region and all the way across North Africa, to trading posts as far away as the Atlantic Ocean. Phoenician cedar was prized for ship building, and the Phoenicians traded with both the Egyptians and the Greeks. However, in 539 BC/BCE, things started to go downhill. First, Cyrus the Great led the Persian army to victory over the Phoenicians, turning Phoenicia into a vassal state. Then, Alexander the Great sacked Tyre after a long siege and the building of an impressive bridge to the fortified city. The Phoenicians fled, many of them landing in Carthage. Although Carthage flourished over the next 150 years or so, Carthage and Rome fought a series of wars called the Punic Wars which ended in Roman victory. Phoenicia itself became absorbed into a Greek kingdom, the Seleucid Kingdom, reaching from the near east into modern day India and western Afghanistan. Finally, the entire region was conquered by the Roman Pompey the Great, becoming the province of Syria in 65 BC/BCE.

Nearby, war raged on as the neo-Babylonian empire fought against Assyrian conquerors, the Egyptians, and then the Persians. The Babylonian king, Nebuchadnezzar II, allegedly built the hanging gardens of Babylon, one of the seven wonders of the ancient world. Egypt, as a vassal state of the Assyrians, fought other wars of expansion during this period and began the construction of a great canal from the Mediterranean to the Red Sea. The Greek city states of Athens and Sparta flourished during the period now described as the Classical Era, with the construction of the Temple of Zeus in Athens and the spreading of Greek culture and language throughout the Mediterranean. The Kingdom of Rome soon fell, becoming the Roman Republic in 509 BC/BCE.

Further away, new world religions sprang into existence while civilizations rose and fell. In Europe, Iron Age Celts settled across the continent in a tribal society,

THE PHOENICIANS

while the Chinese developed a rigid bureaucratic society based on the ideals of Confucianism and Legalism. Taoism was also founded in China, while Buddhism and Jainism were founded in India, and Zoroastrianism was founded in Persia. In the Americas, the majority of cultures were either hunter-gatherers or cultures in the early stages of farming, with the Olmec civilization on decline.

Top: Cover of a Phoenician anthropoid sarcophagus of a woman, made of marble, 350–325 BC, from Sidon, now in the Louvre. Photo by Jebulon.

Bottom: Tharros Roman Ruins, Oristano, Sardinia. Photo by aspence111.

Royal Purple

Ancient Phoenicia was a place where many luxury goods were made and exported—from beautiful, blown glass to papyrus paper. But perhaps the most famous product the Phoenicians produced was the rich purple dye that they made from the Murex ocean snail.

Phoenicians were called the "purple people" because the dye stained the skin of the craftsmen who made it. The dye was made in the city of Tyre by crushing thousands of snails, leaving them to rot in the sun, and then collecting their juices. The whole city stank because of this process. It was an insult in the ancient world to be told that, "You smell like a man from Tyre!" The dye sold for a small fortune in the ancient world, however, so it was probably worth the purple skin and stinkiness to the craftsmen. The reason why purple was considered the color of kings is that only someone as rich as a king could afford it. This made the color purple a status symbol in the ancient world.

Two shells of Bolinus brandaris, the spiny dye-murex, source of the dye. Photo by M. Violante.

The Evolution Of The Alphabet

When you write your letters, have you ever stopped and wondered how they got their shapes? Who first wrote an alphabet? To find the answer, you would have to travel back in time all the way to somewhere between 1900 and 1700 BC/BCE to Egypt and Sinai (a peninsula connecting Egypt and Asia). The people there spoke languages we call "Semitic languages." These were the languages spoken in the Middle East. Some of these languages, like Akkadian (Mesopotamia) and Phoenician are no longer in use. Other Semitic languages are spoken today by millions of people: Aramaic, Hebrew, and Arabic. To get back to our story, a Semitic speaker (or speakers) took Egyptian hieroglyphs and used them to represent sounds. Take the letter "m" for example. The Egyptian hieroglyph for water was a sort of wavy line. It was pronounced "nt." The Semitic speakers took "nt" and pronounced it "mem" in their language. Gradually, the symbol became simply M with the sound we use today. In the first alphabet, called Proto-Sinaic, you can see that the alphabet looks a lot like simple hieroglyphics.

The Phoenicians used this early alphabet, but after a thousand years or so, the lines became simpler and more abstract. The letters don't all face the same way as our modern alphabet, but you can see E, K, L, O, and T if you look closely. This alphabet was a lot easier to learn than complex hieroglyphics, so maybe it was inevitable that the Ancient Greeks would copy this writing system from their trading partners. The Greeks made it even better: they added vowels. (The Phoenicians just figured everyone could add vowel sounds when they read out loud). When you look at the Ancient Greek alphabet, you can really start to see the letters taking a more familiar shape. A, B, and I are all pretty clear now.

Then, the Romans came along. They really liked copying the Greeks (just compare their mythology!) They took the alphabet too, in a language we call Old Latin. They did leave a few letters behind, only using them in Greek words or Roman Numerals: K, X, Y, and Z. There weren't any sounds in Latin that needed those letters. Just like the other alphabets, it changed slowly. A few letters rotated into more recognizable positions. By the time Pompeii was buried underneath volcanic debris, the Latin alphabet looked almost like our alphabet today. It didn't have lowercase letters, and it was still missing a few. J, U, and W are our youngest letters. They were all added to the English language during the Middle Ages. There were also some special letters used in Middle English that have mostly disappeared today, but that's a story for another day.

FURTHER READING

All Ages

Bible Lands by Jonathan N. Tubb. Another one of the DK Eyewitness books, this one covers the Canaanites, the Israelites, and the Phoenicians. This book provides context for the history as well as photographs of historical artifacts. This book is also recommended in the Israelites chapter. Out of print, so check your local library and used book sites.

Ages 5-9

Ancient Israelites and Their Neighbors: An Activity Guide (Cultures of the Ancient World) by Marian Broida. This is the same book recommended for further study of the Israelites. It is one of the few children's books that discusses the Phoenicians. A third of the book is about the Phoenicians and has great and engaging activities such as making purple dye.

Phoenician Glassblowing

Pliny the Elder (who died during the destruction of Pompeii) was a Roman historian. He wrote on many topics, including the Phoenician discovery of glass.

> "A ship belonging to traders in soda once called here, so the story goes, and they spread out along the shore to make a meal. There were no stones to support their cooking-pots, so they placed lumps of soda from their ship under them. When these became hot and fused with the sand on the beach, streams of an unknown liquid flowed, and this was the origin of glass." (Pliny, 362)

Evidence of glass production dates as far back as the 16th century BC/BCE in Mesopotamia, so Pliny might not have the right story. Whether or not this was the true discovery of glass, the Phoenicians were known for their work with this versatile material. They introduced glasswork to the Greek world. They first worked with glass using moulds and cutting tools. Using these techniques, they made bowls and glass tiles used as inlays for mosaics and furniture. Sometimes the glass tiles decorated wooden furniture, sometimes they were placed in ivory pieces. Then, in the middle of the 1st century BC/BCE, the Phoenicians either invented or perfected a game-changing technique: glass blowing. This technique uses a long tube to blow air into molten glass. It was faster and less expensive than earlier glass working techniques. Before glass-blowing, only the wealthy could afford glass objects. Glass-blowing made the material accessible to all people. Glassblowing was also a more versatile technique, allowing the creation of new shapes and objects. Phoenician glass-blowers were barred from travel, but they escaped and carried their techniques throughout the Roman Empire. By the first and second centuries AD/CE, the Phoenicians were making highly decorated and colorful glass pieces. Their pieces have been found in the ashes of Pompeii as well as many other places throughout the ancient world.

How about today? The Maltese people today, descended from the Phoenicians, use techniques and materials much like those of their ancestors.

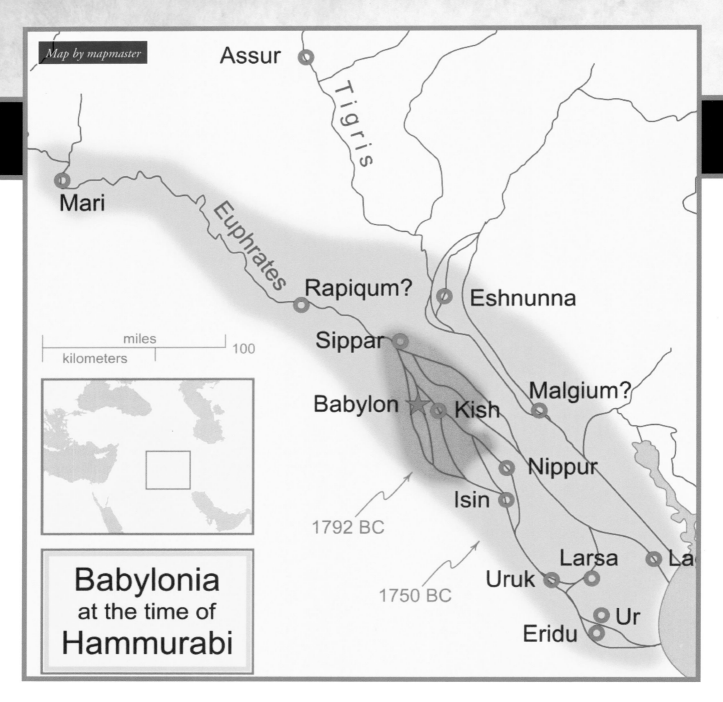

Map by mapmaster

Assur

Tigris

Mari

Euphrates

Rapiqum?

Eshnunna

miles
kilometers
100

Sippar

Malgium?

Babylon ★ Kish

Nippur

Isin

1792 BC

Babylonia
at the time of
Hammurabi

Larsa La

Uruk

1750 BC

Ur

Eridu

Many Christian and Jewish people have heard of Babylon from the book of Genesis in the Bible. According to the story, at a time when everyone in the world spoke the same language, the people in the land of Shinar wished to build a great tower. God saw that with a common language, the people would think that nothing was out of reach, so he made them all speak different languages and caused them to spread out across the earth. As old as this story is, the Babylonian kingdom is centuries older than the time of the Tower of Babel and King

Nebuchadnezzar's Hanging Gardens of Babylon, one of the seven wonders of the Ancient World.

Hammurabi ascended to the throne when his father abdicated, or gave up the throne, at a time when the city had already existed for 1,000 years. Hammurabi united the kingdoms of Mesopotamia into one kingdom, Babylonia, ruled over from the city of Babylon. Located about 60 miles southwest of modern day Baghdad, in Iraq, today waters have risen and covered the oldest parts of the city. However, we know that the city was famous for its temples, and that Hammurabi

BABYLON

turned a minor city into the central city of the kingdom. During his reign, the city was the largest in the world, with a population of more than 200,000 people. His law code still survives today, on a stele displayed at the Louvre Museum in Paris, France. He also created a code of taxation.

When we look at Hammurabi's Code, we get a picture of what life looked like almost 4,000 years ago: surgeons performed operations, veterinarians looked after cattle, the slave trade thrived, and women were generally treated as property. Hammurabi begins his code by stating that these laws were delivered to him by his god, who gave him the right to rule. From that, we know that religion played an important role in Babylonia.

Elsewhere during this period, other civilizations were on the rise. By the end of Hammurabi's reign, Egypt was on its fourteenth dynasty during the period called the Middle Kingdom, and written literature emerged there for the first time. In China, Shang conquest over the Xia dynasty marked the beginning of the Shang Dynasty. The earliest known Chinese writing, on oracle bones, is from this time. On the other hand, the Indus Valley Civilization declined during this century and the Vedic Period began in India. This

was also the last century during which a living species of mammoth, the wooly mammoth, roamed on the earth. The last wooly mammoths lived at the same time as Hammurabi, but far away on Wrangel Island in the Arctic Ocean.

Hammurabi (standing), depicted as receiving his royal insignia from Shamash (or possibly Marduk). Hammurabi holds his hands over his mouth as a sign of prayer[1] (relief on the upper part of the stele of Hammurabi's code of laws). Photo by Mbzt.

Panoramic view of ruins in Babylon photographed in 2005 during a tour for U.S. soldiers.

Archaeology of Babylon

Babylon emerged as a city-state somewhere around 4,000 years ago, and has always been a place of interest to the wider world. Ancient travelers and scholars wrote about the wonders of several Mesopotamian cities, including Babylon, and the city features prominently in several books of the Bible. Ancient writers may have exaggerated some of the height and grandness of the city's features, but the city was a true architectural wonder of its age. Today, historians must sort through ancient documents and the surviving archaeological evidence to try to form a true picture of Babylon's history. How much truth is in these historical documents and stories?

One nineteenth century archaeologist, Heinrich Schliemann, believed that there was historical truth in Homer's Iliad and Odyssey, which led him to try to track down the historic location of the city of Troy. His student, Robert Koldewey, went on to excavate

the ancient ruins of Babylon. Because of Schliemann's influence and because cuneiform translation was in its infancy, many of his interpretations are through the lens of ancient Greek thought. Koldeway believed at one point that he had found the site of the Hanging Gardens of Babylon, one of the Seven Wonders of the Ancient World. Current evidence indicates that these famed gardens either didn't exist or that they were located in the city of Nineveh and he likely uncovered an ancient storeroom. The cuneiform lists of supplies found in the ruins is still an important source, although perhaps slightly less grand than tiered and irrigated gardens. Koldeway also began an excavation of the Ishtar Gate that was completed during the 1930s, at which point the Germans took the bricks back to Berlin to rebuild the gate there. This was not at all unusual. During the first century or so of study, most of the excavations were led by Europeans who took their findings back to Europe. Today, the British Museum owns more than one hundred thousand cuneiform tablets.

In the 1980s, the Iraqi dictator Saddam Hussein ordered excavation and reconstruction at the site of Nebuchadnezzar II's palace. Unfortunately, he did not hire professional archaeologists and preservationists for

the job, and his orders to construct a new palace on top of the old caused further destruction. His orders were politically motivated, to increase his own standing. Many of the bricks were inscribed with the following: "This was built by Saddam, son of Nebuchadnezzar, to glorify Iraq." Further damage happened after Hussein's fall from power, at the hands of American and Polish troops who established a base on top of the ruins. Likewise, civilian looting of the Iraq Museum just before foreign troops arrived resulted in further devastation to the archaeological evidence.

Today, the historical site has guards, tourism has slowly increased and excavations have resumed, but the site of one of the world's oldest cities is still at risk from encroaching development and oil drilling. Only 2% of the city has been excavated, leaving much of the still-buried city at risk. Without further evidence, it is difficult to answer how much is true about ancient descriptions of the city.

Babylon in 1932

Cylinder Seals

In Mesopotamia, civilization evolved so quickly that they developed a need for a bureaucratic system of government before they had even developed a written language. As the government became more organized and complex, the need for a written way to convey official approval and sign legal documents, such as contracts, became evident. How could this be done in a time before a written alphabet? Beginning as early as 3500 BC/BCE, the people of Mesopotamia accomplished this with the use of stone seals, including cylinder seals. These objects became so popular that their use persisted long after writing became commonplace for educated classes.

Cylinder seals were made of stone (often semi-precious stones) or metal, including marble, obsidian, amethyst, lapis lazuli, gold, or silver. A very wealthy person may also have had the seal capped in gold. Additionally, the craftsmanship that went into making the cylinder seals added to the value of the object. A seal cutter apprenticed for four years to learn the delicate art of carving in the negative on an object no more than four inches long. The artists were highly paid for this art, as the carvings were often quite complex images, including full narratives.

In other cases, they were representational of a person. A seal might include symbols representing the person's family, rank, and the owner himself. It's easy to see why such an object might be passed down as an heirloom, but it was also an everyday object. People wore their seals on a leather cord around their neck or wrist, or tied to a garment. And they weren't just for nobles either. Even the lower classes and slaves used cylinder seals, although not made from as fine materials. It's possible that their use persisted for so long after the invention of writing because so many people remained illiterate.

Old Babylonian cylinder seal, hematite. This seal was probably made in a workshop at Sippar (about 40 miles north of Babylon on the map above) either during, or shortly before, the reign of Hammurabi.[15] It depicts the king making an animal offering to the Sun god Shamash.

Linescan camera image of the cylinder seal to the left (reversed to resemble an impression).

Source: Hjaltland Collection

Soap

No one knows exactly how or when soap was invented, but according to a Roman legend, soap was named for Mount Sapo: a place of sacrifice overlooking a river. The fat of the sacrificed animals mixed with wood ash and was washed into the water. Women washing clothing here found that it was easier to clean their garments because of the soap in the water. It's a fun story, but there isn't much evidence that this legend is true. However, it's a good introduction to the chemistry of the soap making process.

Basic soaps have two ingredients: lye, made from soaking ashes, and animal fats or vegetable oils. When the lye and fats come into contact, a chemical reaction happens that turns the two substances into soap. As far as accidental soap making in a river, it seems unlikely. The reaction takes time, with a 24-48 hour incubation and hardening period, followed by air curing for four to six weeks. The curing time is important, since it gives the lye time to deactivate while the rest becomes soap. This deactivation is important, since active lye is extremely caustic when mixed with water. Caustic means that instead of cleaning your skin, it will burn it.

While we don't know how they figured it out, we do know that by around 2800 BC/BCE, people knew how to make soap. The first example of soap discovered by archaeologists was found in ancient Babylon. Soapy substances made of animal fat and ash were discovered inside clay pots and believed to have been used as medicine to treat skin conditions. The soap may also have been used to clean wool and cotton, either as part of the textile industry or to wash clothing. Historians don't know the exact purpose, because while clay tablets have been discovered describing several processes and recipes for soap making, they don't elaborate on the use of the final product. However, soap didn't become an important element of hygiene until thousands of years later.

Although the soap may not have been used to make a person smell better, the Babylonians did love surrounding themselves with scents. They wore perfume and burned incense, and many of these scents were considered both spiritual and medicinal. Juniper and chamomile are herbs grown in the Babylonian region that also may have been used to treat illnesses.

FURTHER READING

All Ages
Color World Culture: Babylonian Art/Phoenician Art by Mrinal Mitra. All of the artwork in this well laid out coloring book is based on artifacts of the Babylonians and the Phoenicians. Younger scholars will enjoy coloring the pictures, while older students can analyze the artwork and make inferences about the culture from the pictured artifacts as a great art history activity. At the end, there is a synopsis for the artwork of each culture.

Ages 5-9
Mesopotamia (True Books: Ancient Civilizations) by Sunita Apte. This simple book covers many Mesopotamian civilizations with wonderful photography, simple text, and interesting facts. It is out of print, so check your local library or look for a used copy.

Ages 10-15
Note: These are the same books used for Uruk because most children's nonfiction books cover all of Mesopotamia.

DK Eyewitness Books: Mesopotamia by Philip Steele. This book covers all of the civilizations in the area, with fantastic illustrations of artifacts from the period. Like all of the Eyewitness books, the illustrations are fantastic for all ages, but the reading level is best for ages ten and up.

Life in Ancient Mesopotamia (Peoples of the Ancient World) by Shilpa Mehta-Jones. This is a great source for daily life, geography, religion, and more with great illustrations and photographs of artifacts.

Arctic

Subarctic

Northwest Coast

Plateau

Northwest Coast

Great Basin

California

Plains

Northeast

Southeast

Southwest

Teotihuacan 100 BC/ BCE-550 AD/CE

Nearly 9,000 years ago, the first people domesticated maize (now usually called corn). They lived in Mexico, and the new crop spread south throughout Central and South America. Maize was able to support a dense population, and civilizations grew. Several developed into urban centers with monumental structures. One of these ancient cities is called Teotihuacan, and by 500 AD/CE,

it was the largest city in the Americas and the 6th largest city in the world. Over 125,000 people called it home and it sprawled over eight square miles. The name comes from an Aztec term that translates roughly to "birthplace of the gods." This name was given to the ruins hundreds of years after the city had been abandoned. We don't know exactly what its original residents called their home. The Maya called it Puh, or "place of reeds."

The city was a busy place. Channels provided a route for canoes carrying food from farms to places all around the city. Large pyramids like the Pyramid of the

NORTH AMERICAN CIVILIZATIONS

Sun were used for religious ceremonies, but Teotihuacan was more than just a religious center. It was also a home. Many people lived in huge compounds that housed sixty or more families, something like single story apartment buildings. Some of the poorest inhabitants of the city lived in adobe huts. People from all over Mesoamerica came to the city, and it shared many characteristics with cultures from the south. People in Teotihuacan played the same ball game played by the Olmecs and worshipped similar gods such as a Maize Goddess and Rain God.

The Pyramid of the Sun is the largest pyramid in the city and the third largest pyramid of any kind in the world, but it's not the only impressive pyramid. The Pyramid of the Feathered Serpent kept its remarkable treasures secret for hundreds of years, until a series of heavy storms in 2003 created a sinkhole. An archaeologist named Gomez Chavez realized that the sinkhole revealed a shaft. He knew there was a tunnel under the Pyramid of the Sun and thought there might be

a similar tunnel made accessible by the shaft. He was right about the tunnel, and when they cleared away the debris they found tens of thousands of artifacts. The archaeologists found jade jaguars as well as bones from real jaguars. They also found a miniature landscape with lakes made of liquid mercury. The walls and ceiling were painted with a mixture of pyrite, magnetite, and hematite. In its full glory, the passage would have sparkled brilliantly. All of the artifacts seem to have been offerings for the gods.

While Teotihuacan is located in North America, it has far more in common with civilizations to the south than those to the north. Why is that? One theory: maize. Maize, usually called corn in the United States, spread south from Mexico. It grew well throughout Mesoamerica and traveled down into the Andean Mountains in Peru. Because it grew so well and fed so many people, it allowed a higher number of people to live close together. It took longer to spread to the rest of North America and there was only one other

Left side view of the Pyramid of the Sun.
Photo by Wernervp.

indigenous grain (wild rice). When it did, populations increased. The population of the Mississippian city of Cahokia went from thousands to tens of thousands after the introduction of maize in around 1000 AD/CE. Hunter-gatherers in North America started to settle down to grow maize, but they made the transition from hunting and gathering to agriculture much later than their southern neighbors just because of the availability of maize.

Ancestral Puebloans 1500 BC/BCE to 50 AD/CE

When it comes to history, names can be confusing. Sometimes, people who have written languages leave enough records for historians to know what they called themselves. But sometimes, historians have to use clues to figure out the name of a long ago culture. Have you ever heard of the Anasazi people? They were people who lived in Utah, Arizona, New Mexico, and Colorado. The name "Anasazi" comes from a Navajo term meaning "ancient enemies." Anthropologists and historians used this term for many years. However, the Pueblo people who descended from the Anasazi prefer term "Ancestral Puebloans" to refer to these ancient people. Modern anthropologists have adopted the term preferred by the Pueblo. The earliest Ancestral Puebloan culture is called the Basketmaker Culture, named for the extensive baskets they left behind. The Basketmakers had no known written language but their closest descendants, the Hopi people, called them Hisatsinom or "ancient people."

They were semi-nomadic hunter-gatherers who supplemented their diet with...maize! They started growing maize around 500 BC/BCE. Unlike more settled agrarian societies, they planted the corn in the spring and then traveled during the growing season. Then they returned for the harvest. Because of this fairly unique system, they did not build large settlements. Instead they lived in cave shelters in the earliest days of their culture. Eventually, they started building pit houses. In Arizona, road workers discovered a site with two pit houses when they were digging out the ground for new road construction. The two houses were large ovals and had smaller pits used for cooking and heating as

Ruins of Pueblo Bonito, in Chaco Canyon. Photo by Toran Tarzan.

well as storage pits. The residents had brought in river cobbles to line the cooking pits because they absorb heat. The fire was built on top of the river cobbles and then they used smaller stones to boil water in baskets. First, the stones were heated in a fire, and then dropped into a basket full of water. Because the region was so dry, these river cobbles came from some distance away. Archaeologists found quite a few artifacts, include stone spear tips. For most of the Basketmaker period, hunters used spears and a spear thrower called an atlatl. Bows and arrows came later. The people who lived in the pit houses must also have eaten some grain because of the metate and manos found at the site. These were stones used for grinding. Probably ten to twenty people lived there in a seasonal camp. They carved stone and bone, and collected stones that resembled things like people or animals. What did they wear? They made sandals out of fibers from the yucca plant, jewelry made from shells, and robes made of feathers and fur. Later on, pit houses were built closer together as the people started living in small villages.

By 300 AD/CE, the Basketmakers fully relied on maize and had started to use pottery in place of baskets. New varieties of more productive corn were introduced over the next several centuries and the population grew. By 750 AD/CE, the Basketmaker culture had changed so much that a new era began: the Pueblo era. The Pueblo lived in above-ground houses and had left their hunting and gathering ways behind. Villages grew to hundreds of people.

Pot from Kolomoki Mounds. Photo by Bubba73.

The Woodland Period

If you look at a map of Europe today, you can see that Europe is made up of many smaller countries. Until Europeans started arriving and making their own borders, North America was the same way. We don't know exactly how many nations lived in North America but today there are more than 600 tribes with either federal or state recognition. Another 400 or more are considered "unrecognized tribes."[1] So, let's say there are still at least 1000 tribes today. Imagine each one of these as its own country. They had their own leaders, their own languages, and their own traditions. Just like today French, Spanish, Italian, and Portuguese are part of the same language family, North America had its own language families. Today, the European Union connects countries throughout Europe. Hundreds of years ago, vast trade networks spanned the continent of North America. Think of it this way: sometimes, we group European countries together if they have a lot in common with each other. The British Isles, the Mediterranean, and Scandinavia are all regions in Europe with similar cultures but with distinct identities. Historians use the term "Woodland Indians" to describe the indigenous cultures of the eastern United States starting in 1000 BC/BCE. The Woodland Period lasted until about 1000 AD/CE. Just like we can't generalize about all the people in different European countries, we can't make too many generalizations about the people of this region, since there were many distinct cultures with different languages and traditions. However, there were certain shared characteristics.

- Pottery was universal. What did it look like? Different regions had different styles. The photo to the left is an example of one.
- They were starting to transition from nomadic to permanent settlements. Some were beginning to farm. Maize arrived right around 1000 AD/CE, and more and more groups started raising maize and other crops in addition to hunting and gathering.
- Widespread trade networks. Can you imagine goods traveling from Florida to Maine just by the power of people's feet? There were no cars,

1. Recognition is a complicated issue. Some tribes had recognized status and lost it. Others have been denied recognition. The reasons are too complex to go into here.

trains, or airplanes of course. The horse had not yet arrived in the Americas, so everything was carried by people.

- Mound building, or the use of earth to build monumental platforms, had begun even earlier in North America and continued for thousands of years.

Here are two of the oldest Woodland cultures:

The Adena Culture

From about 1000 BC/BCE to 200 BC/BCE, in the Ohio Valley and surrounding areas, there lived a people that we call the Adena Culture. This name came from the estate where one of their burial mounds is located. The name was given in the 19th century because the Adena people left no record of what they called themselves and we have no clues from any other people at the time. We don't know how groups in the Adena culture were structured, but the name is used to describe a set of people with shared traditions and similar artifacts. Like some other North American cultures, they built large mounds out of earth as part of their burial rituals. During burial rituals, the dead were burned and then covered in dirt to create the mounds. Archaeologists have found grave goods inside the mounds, helping us to make hypotheses about the Adena. They carved geometric and animal designs into stone tablets, which were possibly used to stamp designs onto fabric or their bodies. They made jewelry and ritual clothing out of copper and animal bones and antlers. Copper, which was found in surface deposits, was hammered into desired shapes. It was mostly used for decoration, while tools were made of stone. They also

FURTHER READING

All Ages
Indian Life in Pre-Columbian North America: Coloring Book by John Green. From prehistory to more well-known nations, this coloring book has a little bit of everything. It has several pages on mound-building cultures.

Ages 5-9
Stones, Bones, and Petroglyphs: Digging into Southwest Archaeology by Susan E. Goodman. While this book focuses on the Pueblo period, which is after the Basketmakers, it's a great read. A group of students accompanies professional archaeologists on a dig. They learn about best practices, respect for the descendants of the people they are studying, and how archaeology can help us understand how people lived long ago.

Ages 10-15

The following books are out of print. However, used copies are available and you can always check your local library or used book dealer. There are limited options for children about this period.

City of the Gods: Mexico's Ancient City of Teotihuacan by Caroline Arnold. This book covers the importance of the people of Teotihuacan to surrounding cultures, information about their daily lives, and a description of the city.

Pyramid of the Sun, Pyramid of the Moon by Leonard Everett Fisher. (On Amazon, Angela Fisher is listed as the author). This book is written on the premise that the people of Teotihuacan were the Toltecs, but that's up for debate. It's on the list because it's a slightly simpler text and more narrative than *City of the Gods*. Fisher takes the story all the way up through the Aztecs to the arrival of the Spanish.

The Anasazi by Eleanor H. Ayer. While this book uses the older term for Ancestral Puebloans, it is a readable and descriptive volume. The first 30 pages or so are focused on the Basketmaker period.

left behind pottery, although these were not part of the burial offerings.

The Adena were mostly hunter-gatherers, although they grew some crops as well. They lived in small settlements near the mounds. Their wooden houses were circular and covered with bark.

The Hopewell Tradition or Hopewell Culture

This group was actually not a single culture or people, but a collection of social groups that lived from 100 BC/BCE to 500 AD/CE and ran from Florida to Canada, from the East Coast to the Midwest. They were connected by a network of trade routes using waterways. It's possible that some groups grew out of the Adena Culture.

Unlike the Adena, in the Hopewell Tradition, the dead were usually cremated while mound burials were reserved for only the most important members of society. Sometimes, these were the most skilled hunters. Other times, they were most likely leaders chosen for their talents or their ability to persuade followers. Later, these positions would evolve into the chiefs of Native American tribes. The mounds where these leaders were buried served more than one purpose. Many of them were shaped like animals, while others are arranged according to astronomical events like moon phases and solstices.

The Hopewell peoples had their own artistic traditions. The trade network allowed precious materials like mica, pearls, copper, and silver to travel over great distances. They also had a talent for carving. Their smoking pipes were often shaped like animals and birds. One mask was made out of a human skull, and other carvings made of human bone have been found.

At the end of the Hopewell period, mound building came to an end and the trade network no longer connected people thousands of miles apart. Why did this happen? Some archaeologists believe that wars broke out, forcing them to focus on building up their defenses instead of making art and trading. It could also have been related to climate change or over-hunting as a result of the introduction of the bow and arrow.

What about maize? We don't see it in most of this region until about 1000 years ago. Just 500 years later, Europeans began settling in the Americas. While the people of Mesoamerica had an 8000 year head start on maize, there just wasn't time for large populations to develop before everything changed. Is this why we don't see the remains of big cities in North America?

In the rest of the world, wheat, barley, and rice were the grains of choice. Wheat played a major role in Greek and Roman religion, just like maize was central to American religion. Rice played a similar role in Asian countries like China and Japan. Every major civilization has its staple food. What is the staple food in your home? (Hint: a staple food would be a dish or ingredient that you eat nearly daily).

Pot with a bird design, Hopewell site. Photo by Deborah Platt.

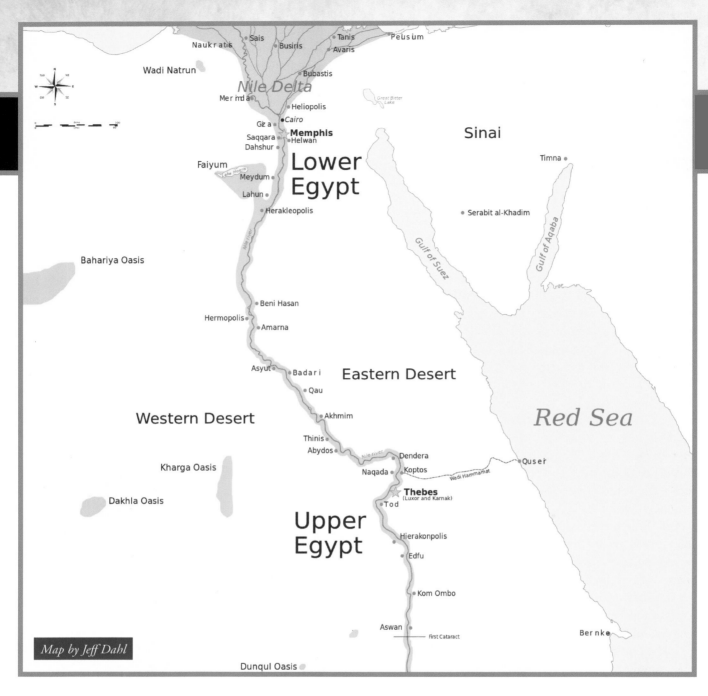

Map by Jeff Dahl

How ancient is Ancient Egypt? This might give you a general idea. In total, Egypt had 34 dynasties... all before the Romans conquered the nation in 30 BC/BCE. The 4th Dynasty existed during the Old Kingdom of Egypt, a prosperous time in Egypt's history. The kingdom expanded up the Nile River (remember, the Nile River runs south to north!), into what is Sudan today. The recently completed Great Pyramid of Giza wasn't Egypt's first pyramid–the earliest pyramids, called mastabas, were "bench" pyramids. Step pyramids were the next innovation in pyramid technology, and the first "true" pyramid was the Red Pyramid of Dashur. Along

with the Great Pyramid, the Sphinx was probably built during the 4th dynasty.

According to the Greek historian Herodotus, the pyramids were built largely by slave labor. However, historians now believe that most of the work was performed by peasants and skilled workers from across the kingdom. Peasants could not work in their fields during the flooding season, so they spent this time working on the pyramids. Historians figured this out through records excavated from overseers' tombs and other writings from the time period.

EGYPT

During the 5th dynasty, trade expanded and temples were built for the worship of the sun god, Ra. Pharaohs would rule Egypt until the Roman invasion. In fact, more years passed between the building of the Great Pyramid and the birth of the famous Egyptian Queen Cleopatra than have passed since Cleopatra's time until now.

Meanwhile, two nearby regions were growing rapidly: the Near East and South Asia. Both regions were in the Bronze Age, with evidence of writing and rapidly growing urban centers along with skilled working of bronze. Their populations were specialized (citizens had specific skills and professions), and their armies became stronger. The kingdom of Sumer, in what is now Iraq and Iran grew during this period. The Indus Valley Civilization was flourishing. Egypt, Mesopotamia (Sumer), and the Indus Valley Civilization made up the three old world civilizations.

Most of Europe was still in the Copper Age (Bronze Age technology involved the alloy of copper and other metals, and was therefore more advanced). Ancient Greece and the Roman Empire would not come into existence for centuries. In China, several different cultures developed across what was not yet a united China. The cultivation of cereal crops was a relatively new invention. On the continent of Africa, cultural advances centered around the Red Sea and Eastern Mediterranean, with distinct cultures some 500 years in the future in Central and West Africa. In the Americas, the oldest American civilization, the Norte Chico civilization, flourished. The Norte Chico civilization, located in what is now Peru, predated the Olmec civilization by roughly two thousand years.

Overall, much of what we take for granted in our culture today had not even been invented yet. Most of the world did not yet farm; money was a new and rare concept, and tools were rudimentary. The three old civilizations: Mesopotamia, the Indus Valley civilization, and the ancient Egyptians paved the way in culture and science, setting groundwork for the rest of the world to follow.

Face of the Great Sphinx with Pyramids in the background. Photo by pius99.

The Builders

The Pyramids at Giza were one of the Seven Wonders of the World in ancient times, and the only one of the ancient wonders still in existence. While the three great pyramids are architecturally spectacular, the story of the building of the pyramid complex is equally as impressive. In addition to the three large pyramids, there are seven smaller queen's pyramids, numerous tombs, boat pits, temples, and, of course, the Sphinx. More recent excavations have uncovered "pyramid towns" near the pyramids–places where skilled laborers lived while they worked on the pyramids. It took 10,000 laborers about 30 years to build a pyramid, working in three month shifts.

The busiest building time was during the Nile's flood season, when farmers could not work their fields and needed other work. The laborers, who were not slaves, not only received pay, but also food and clothing. The worker's town had a hospital, cemetery, and breweries. Nearby agricultural settlements provided meat and other food for the workers. Given the intense physical nature of the work, the workers required high volumes of protein and consumed more than 4,000 pounds of meat per day. The overseers ate beef, the most desirable type of meat, while lower workers ate sheep and goat meat. The number of herders required to maintain enough animals to feed the army of builders amounted to around 2% of Egypt's population at the time! The animals grazing space covered an area equal to the size of Los Angeles. And that's just the meat! In addition, the workers consumed large amounts of grain, beer, fish, beans, and lentils.

The towns were largely inhabited by more skilled workers, while laborers may have lived in camps next to the pyramids that were mostly just shelters from the sun. Overall, though, the workers must have been pleased with their treatment, for later folk tales featured the generosity of the pharaoh to his workers. Many of them were buried in mud-brick tombs near their greatest work.

Mummies

You can't talk about ancient Egypt without talking about mummies. But did you know that mummies have existed all over the world since ancient times? A mummy is a body whose skin and organs have been preserved. Sometimes, they happen naturally. The Ice Man, Ötzi, was a man in the Alps whose body was preserved by ice and dry weather conditions. In the United Kingdom, Germany, and some Scandinavian countries, bodies were buried in bogs. The bogs provided the perfect conditions natural mummification. In ancient Iran, a salt mine collapse created natural mummies. In 19th century Pennsylvania, the body of a woman dubbed "The Salt Lady" was naturally preserved when bacteria and and moisture combined in a chemical reaction that created a waxy substance called adipocere. Adipocere prevents any further decomposition and preserves the body just like other forms of natural mummification. Originally, the ancient Egyptians buried the bodies of their dead in the sand. The dry desert stands mummified the bodies naturally. Then, the Egyptians began mummifying their dead on purpose.

There were three processes for mummification in Egypt. Families chose the most thorough and expensive method they could afford. Otherwise, they were afraid that their loved one might come back to haunt them. According to ancient Greek historians, in the first, and most expensive, method, the brain was removed through the nostrils. Then the skull was washed out and the brain discarded. The priests then cut open the body cavity. The heart was left in the body, but the rest of the organs were removed. Canopic jars made of pottery or stone held the stomach, intestines, liver, and lungs. Then the priests poured aromatic oils and resins into the body and covered the whole body in natron salt for seventy days. At the end of that period, the fully preserved body was washed and wrapped in linen strips stuck on with gum resin. The family took the body and buried it, usually in a wooden mummy case. Royal mummies were stored in elaborate sarcophagi and placed in tombs. Priests using the second method injected the body with cedar oil and buried the body in natron salt for seventy days. The oil liquified the organs, which could then be drained. In the final, most economical, method, the body was simply washed and stored in natron for the same seventy-day period. At least, that's what the Greeks said. Researchers who studied 150 actual mummies found a lot more variation and no use of cedar oil. In some cases, both the brain and heart were left intact. What can we learn? There was likely a great deal of variation between mummy workshops across Egypt and throughout the long era of ritual mummification.

Why did the Egyptians preserve their bodies this way? They believed that people needed their bodies in the afterlife and mummification allowed the soul to recognize the body. They considered the heart the center of the soul and so left it in the body. They also buried their dead with all the goods they would need in the afterlife, including combs, jewelry, food and drink, clothing, and favorite objects. They also mummified animals like cats, dogs, gazelles, baboons, and sacred bulls. Over a million Egyptian mummies have been discovered, and more than two hundred thousand were animals. During the early days of Egyptian archaeology, many mummies were exported as curios and even ground into powder and sold as medicines or as a pigment to make a paint color called "mummy brown." Others made it into museums around the world.

Egyptians weren't the only ancient culture to use ritual mummification. The Inca, the Aztec, the Maori, the Australian Aborigines, and the Torres Strait people all mummified their dead during certain periods. Do people still mummify the dead? Not typically but there are a few exceptions. In Papua New Guinea, the Anga people have practiced mummification for thousands of years. The practice is no longer common, but tribe elders are still sometimes mummified.

How about the famous mummy's curse? Occasionally, tombs have inscriptions meant to protect the tomb. These inscriptions could be viewed as curses, but aren't intended for tomb robbers. Instead they were intended to preserve the purity of the tomb. Most of these are from Egypt's Old Kingdom. Most of the fears about cursed tombs come from imaginative 19th century Europeans. Louisa May Alcott, famous for her *Little Women* book series, wrote the first known work of fiction featuring a mummy curse plot. It's called *Lost in a Pyramid, or The Mummy's Curse.* Believers in curses often refer to the deaths of several members of Howard Carter's team who entered Tutankhamun's tomb. However, most of the members of the expedition lived long lives and died under perfectly normal circumstances. Carter himself never believed in a curse.

If all this got you interested in being mummified yourself someday, start saving your pennies. Modern mummification costs about $67,000. Is it worth it? Only you can decide.

Egyptian Food & Drink

If you travelled back to Ancient Egypt, what would be on the menu? Well, that depends on your social standing and when you traveled to. After all, Ancient Egyptian history spans thousands of years. It's safe to say, however, that if you were visiting during the reign of any pharaoh, you would be offered beer to drink. Yes, even if you were a child! Both adults and children drank beer. Beer and bread formed the central part of the Ancient Egyptian diet, and provided essential amino acids in a somewhat sparse diet (for the lower class). Wages were paid in beer, and beer was an important part of offerings to the gods. But this is not the beer most adults are familiar with today. It was cloudy and had solid sprouted grain floating in it. It also had a lower alcohol content than most modern beers. And it contained tetracycline, an antibiotic that wouldn't be available for thousands of years. So it's quite possible that Ancient Egyptian beer played an important role in Egyptian health!

What else did the Egyptians eat besides beer and bread? Well, they ate some fruits and vegetables you might find familiar: celery, lettuce, scallions (green onions), cucumbers, melons, grapes, figs, and dates. They also ate papyrus! For meat, wealthy Egyptians ate beef while the less wealthy ate goat, sheep, and some pork. Almost everyone ate fish, given their proximity to the Nile. One dish you probably haven't tried is roasted hedgehog. They wrapped the whole hedgehog in clay and baked it. When they broke off the clay, it pulled off all the spines and voila! Dinner is served.

FURTHER READING

All Ages

Treasury of Egyptian Mythology by Donna Jo Napoli. This book from National Geographic has wonderfully written narratives of the best tales from Egyptian mythology accompanied by gorgeous illustrations.

The Mummy Makers of Egypt by Tamara Bower. Bower is a professional archaeological illustrator and scholar of hieroglyphs. She turns her talents to a family of embalmers and their important customers.

Ages 5-9

Hieroglyphs by Joyce Milton. Readers will learn about more than just hieroglyphs, although this book is a fantastic introduction. They will also learn about scribes, mythology, and school.

Ages 10-15

The 5,000-Year-Old Puzzle by Claudia Logan. Tomb Giza 7000X is the oldest royal burial site uncovered in Egypt, as old as the pyramids. But who was buried there? This picture book is both a mystery and a tutorial in archaeology through the eyes of a young boy on the expedition.

Egyptian Games

One of the wonderful things about studying Ancient Egypt is that the Egyptians left behind so much information. Between hieroglyphs, wall paintings, and tombs fully stocked for the afterlife, we are able to learn a great deal about daily life in Egypt, including how they spent their leisure time. Games were an important part of life in Egypt, and the oldest known game was called Senet. In the British Museum in London, visitors can look at a Senet set dating back to 5500-3100 BC/BCE, even before the Pharaohs. They played more than just Senet. Other board games included Dogs and Jackals (with a board that looks a little like a modern cribbage board) and Mehen, a game played on a board resembling a coiled up snake. Children also played a game similar to modern checkers. The ancient Egyptians also enjoyed games and activities familiar to us today, such as tug of war, handball, floor hockey, archery, horse racing, boxing, and long distance running.

In addition to games and sports, Egyptian children had toys. They had dolls made of papyrus and cloth, toy hippopotamuses made of wood with jaws that opened and shut, clay rattles shaped like animals or people, and balls made of papyrus or leather. They also spent most of their time outdoors, playing in the river or wrestling with each other. And both children and adults enjoyed dancing!

All of this evidence indicates that Egyptian children and the children of today would find much common ground in their games.

Painting in tomb of Egyptian Queen Nefertari (1295–1255 BC). Source: The Yorck Project.

THE GIRL WITH THE ROSE-RED SLIPPERS

Long ago in Egypt there lived a wealthy Greek merchant named Charaxos. He spent most of his life trading in Egypt, and his wealth had become vast. In his old age he settled in Naucratis, not far from the mouth of the Nile.

One day, when he was walking in the marketplace, he saw a great crowd gathered. Out of curiosity he pushed his way into their midst, and found that everyone was looking at a slave girl who was about to be sold. She was obviously a Greek; with white skin and cheeks like blushing roses, and Charaxos caught his breath for he had never seen anyone so lovely. Consequently, when the bidding began, Charaxos determined to buy her and, being one of the wealthiest merchants in all Naucratis, he did so easily.

When he had bought the girl, he discovered that her name was Rhodopis and that she had been carried away by pirates from her home in the north of Greece when she was a child. She had grown up in slavery, but had the good fortune of kind masters and a true friend: an ugly little man called Aesop who was always kind to her and told her the most entrancing stories and fables about animals and birds and human beings.

Charaxos listened to her tale and wanted to give her a better life. Instead of treating her as a slave, he looked on her as a daughter. He gave her a lovely house to live in, with a garden in the middle of it, and slave girls to attend her. He lavished her with gifts of jewels and beautiful clothes, including a pair of lovely rose-red slippers. Rhodopis enjoyed these luxuries immensely and was quite contented until, one day, a strange thing happened.

Rhodopis was bathing in the marble-edged pool in her secret garden, for a summer's day even in the north of Egypt grows very hot about noon. Suddenly, when all seemed quiet and peaceful, an eagle came out of the blue sky. It ignored the startled Rhodopis and her servants and instead swooped right down and picked up one of the rose-red slippers in its talons. Then it soared up into the air again on its great wings and, still carrying the slipper, flew away to the south over the valley of the Nile. Rhodopis wept at the loss of her rose-red slipper, sure that she would never see it again.

But the eagle seemed to have been sent by the gods - perhaps by Horus himself, whose sacred bird he was - for he flew straight up the Nile and then swooped down towards the palace. At that hour Pharaoh Amasis was sitting in the great courtyard administering to his people and hearing any complaints that they wished to bring. Down over the courtyard swooped the eagle and dropped the rose-red slipper of Rhodopis into Pharaoh's lap.

The people cried out in surprise when they saw this, and Amasis too was much taken aback. But, as he took up the little rose-red slipper and admired the delicate workmanship and the tiny size of it, he felt that the girl for whose foot it was made must indeed be one of the loveliest in the world.

Indeed, Amasis the Pharaoh was so moved by what had happened that he issued a decree:

"Let my messengers go forth through all the cities of the Delta and, if need be, into Upper Egypt to the very borders of my kingdom. Let them take with them this rose-red slipper which the divine bird of Horus has brought to me, and let them declare that her from whose foot this slipper came shall be the bride of Pharaoh!"

Then the messengers prostrated themselves crying, "Life, health, strength be to Pharaoh! Pharaoh has spoken and his command shall be obeyed!"

So they set forth from Memphis and went by way of Heliopois and Tanis and Canopus until they came to Naucratis. Here they heard of the rich merchant Charaxos and of how he had bought the beautiful Greek girl in the slave market, and how he was lavishing all his wealth upon her as if she had been a princess put in his care by the gods.

So they went to the great house beside the Nile and found Rhodopis in the quiet garden beside the pool.

When they showed her the rose-red slipper she cried out in surprise that it was hers. She held out her foot so that they could see how well it fitted her; and she bade one of the slave girls fetch the matching slipper, which she had kept carefully in memory of her strange adventure with the eagle.

Then the messengers knew that this was the girl whom Pharaoh had sent them to find, and they knelt before her and said, "The good god Pharaoh Amasis - life, health, strength be to him! - bids you come with all speed to his palace at Memphis. There you shall be treated with all honor and given a high place in his Royal House of Women: for he believes that Horus, the son of Isis and Osiris, sent the eagle to bring the rose-red slipper and cause him to search for you."

Such a command could not be disobeyed. Rhodopis bade farewell to Charaxos, who was torn between joy at her good fortune and sorrow at his loss, and set out for Memphis.

And when Amasis saw her beauty, he was sure that the gods had sent her to him. He did not merely take her into his Royal House of Women, he made her his Queen and the Royal Lady of Egypt. And they lived happily together for the rest of their lives.

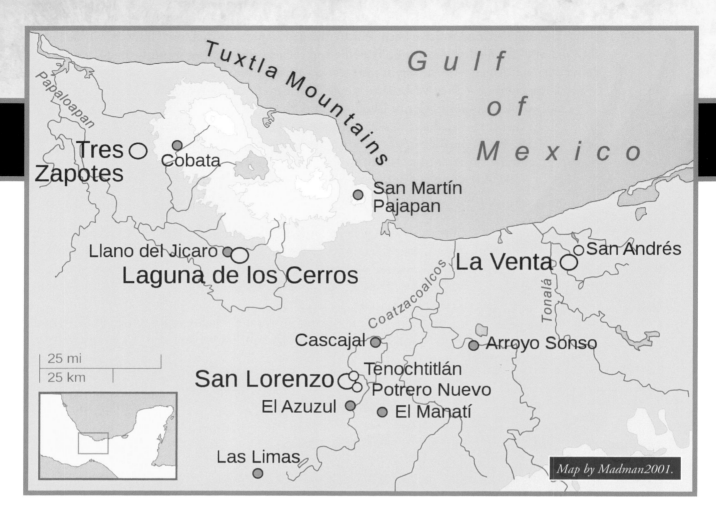

The Olmec were one of the first civilizations in the Americas and the first major civilization in modern-day Mexico. People had already lived in the Americas for thousands of years, but had not come together to form a complex civilization before the Olmecs. The Olmec civilization lasted a thousand years before a sharp drop in population led to its decline in the fourth century BC/BCE. From the origin of the civilization to the cause of the population decline, much of Olmec history has been swallowed up by the jungle with only some of the written history surviving on carved stones. Mainstream consensus is that the Olmec civilization

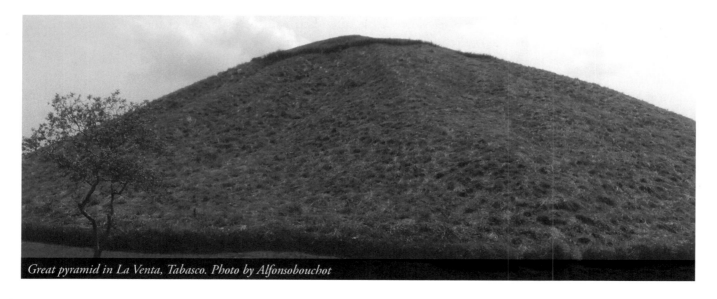

Great pyramid in La Venta, Tabasco. Photo by Alfonsobouchot

THE OLMECS

arose entirely out of indigenous influences, but the lack of strong evidence and the aura of mystery around the civilization has led others to come up with "Olmec Alternative Origin Speculations." (Google the term to read some interesting, but likely inaccurate, theories). In the end, the population decline likely occurred due to environmental factors or tropical diseases, but we cannot know for sure based on current evidence.

We do know that Olmec culture influenced two other empires coming to power at the same time: the Mayan and Aztec civilizations. Olmec civilization influenced the writing, culture, and architecture of these groups. The Olmecs had a wide trade influence along the Gulf coast, and their ball game spread across Mesoamerica and the Caribbean.

Around the world, empires rose and fell during the thousand year reign of the Olmecs. In 976 BC/BCE, King Solomon became the anointed king of Israel, the Mesoamerican empire of the Zapotecs began in 850 BC/BCE and in 814 BC/BCE, Carthage was founded. The next century brought the first Olympiad and the founding of Rome. The once mighty Assyrian empire fell in 631 BC/BCE. Buddhism entered the religious scene in 528 BC/BCE. During the years of the early 5th century, Greece and Persia fought many wars, including the famed battles of Marathon and Thermopylae. Another civilization arose in the Americas in 350 BC/BCE: the Nasca in Peru. And around the same time, Alexander the Great was said to have conquered the "Known World." Little did he know that his great empire arose just as America's oldest civilization came to an end.

Olmec-style mask from Tabasco (Mexico). Musées Royaux d'Art et d'Histoire, Brussels (Belgium). Photo by Michel wal.

Head of Olmeca in Villhermosa Museum. Photo by Glysiak.

FURTHER READING

All Ages
Books about the Olmecs for children are scarce, but books about pre-Columbian Mesoamerican civilizations often contain some information.

Rain Player by David Wisniewsky. While this book is a Mayan tale about a boy who plays the Mesoamerican ball game against a god, it fits with the Olmec because of their influence on Mayan culture. The cut paper illustrations are absolutely beautiful.

Life in Ancient Mesoamerica by Lynn Peppas. While this book makes broad generalizations across the Olmec, Maya, and Aztec cultures, it does give a basic overview of the Olmec and their influence on subsequent civilizations. For sensitive learners, be aware of the graphically illustrated section on Blood Sacrifices, found on pages 22-23. You can easily skip these if needed by paperclipping the pages together.

Olmec Firsts

As the first known Mesoamerican civilization, the Olmecs had a powerful influence on later cultures, both in Mesoamerica and the world at large. Here are some of their firsts:

1. Rubber
   They invented rubber. The name Olmec is actually the Aztec word for "rubber people." The Olmec people learned how to process latex harvested from local trees into rubber.

2. Fun and Games
   Rubber came in handy in the first Mesoamerican ball game, played in a ballcourt with rubber balls.

3. Chocolate Fever
   If you enjoy chocolate, you can thank the Olmecs, who were the first to drink (yes, drink) chocolate.

4. Jaguars, Eagles, and Snakes, Oh My!
   Olmec religion influenced the religious practices of later Mesoamerican civilizations. They had temple mounds, worshipped multiple gods (many were animals), and possibly engaged in human sacrifice.

5. Dates
   They may have invented a calendar that inspired later Mesoamerican civilizations, like the Maya.

6. Written Down
   Olmecs created the first writing system in the Americas.

7. The Price is Right
   They developed the first trade network in the Americas, stretching from Mexico to modern-day Nicaragua. Olmec artifacts, such as figurines, have been found as far as 400 miles away from the center of their civilization.

8. Pyramids
   The Olmecs built the first pyramids in America. They were step pyramids.

9. Getting a Head
   The most famous artifacts left by the Olmecs are their monumental heads--and yes, they were the first to have monumental (large) sculptures in the Americas.

Latex being collected from a tapped rubber tree. Photo by PRA.

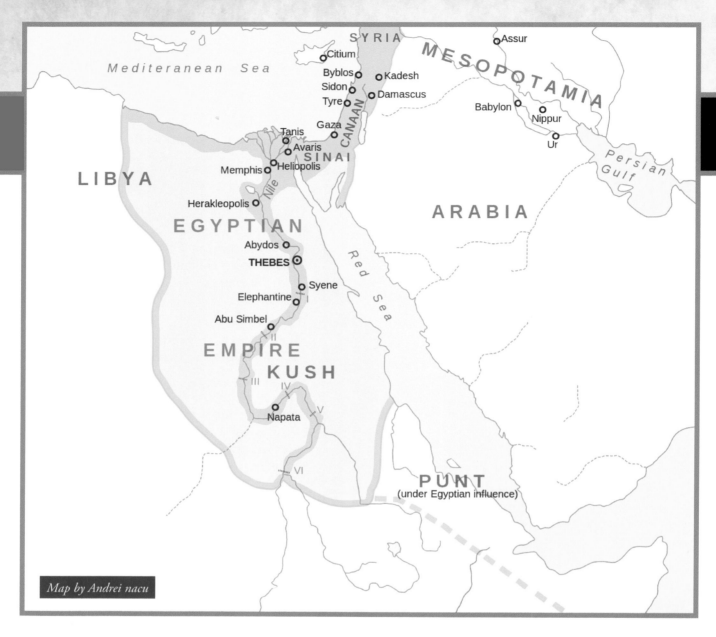

Map by Andrei nacu

Thousands of years ago, the ancient Egyptians wrote about a magical kingdom called Punt. They called it *Ta netjer*, "The Land of the Gods," and believed it was their ancestral homeland. To Akhenaten, Nefertiti, and Tutankhamun, Punt was no more than a legend. But to the famous female pharaoh Hatshepsut, it represented her greatest triumph. She traveled there on an expedition, one considered long and dangerous. Where was this magical kingdom? Today, scholars debate the exact location. Many believe Punt was located in today's Puntland State of Somalia, an independent region of Somalia.

In 1493 BC/BCE, Hatshepsut sailed down the Nile with an expedition carrying jewelry, tools, and weapons for trade. After sailing upriver (south) for some time, they dismantled the boats and carried everything over land to the Red Sea. Carefully hugging the coast in their boats, the Egyptians made their way south once more until they arrived in Punt. It must have been a grand adventure, for the Egyptians were not a seafaring people. The people of Punt were surprised to receive visitors, for they thought they lived at the ends of the earth. The king and queen of Punt gave Hatshepsut and her fellow travelers a warm welcome. In exchange for Egyptian goods, the people of Punt traded gold, ebony, ivory, wild apes, and frankincense trees. When Hatshepsut brought the living trees back to Egypt and planted them near a temple, she carried out the first known successful attempt to transplant foreign plants. These trees lived for centuries, and their roots can still be seen today. Hatshepsut's expedition was not the first

PUNT

or last Egyptian expedition to Punt, merely the most famous. Egyptians had traded with Punt from at least as early as 2613 BC/BCE and Egyptians continued to travel to Punt until around 1155 BC/BCE. The Egyptians described the ways in which Punt measured the length of a year, shifting from a lunar to solar calendar. Punt was home to carpenters, stonemasons, architects, shipbuilders, and weavers. For unknown reasons, trade with Punt ceased and the kingdom became no more than a myth.

About a thousand years later, trade with the Horn of Africa had resumed. We know from ancient Greek writers that a series of city-states in modern-day Somalia formed part of a trade network connecting the Mediterranean region with Arabia and India. City-states like Mosylun, Opone (possibly Punt!), Malao, Sarapion, Mundus, and Essina traded with Phoenicia, Egypt, Greece, Persia, and even the Roman Empire. When Arab traders banned Indian traders from their ports, the Somalian kingdoms welcomed these traders and bought their cargo of cinnamon and other spices. Then they passed it off as their own product and sold it to merchants in North Africa, the Near East, and Europe. The Somali kingdoms were also the main suppliers of frankincense, myrrh, and spices to these regions. The merchants sailed on fast ships called *beden,* which are still in use today. They sailed up and down the Red Sea and may have even occasionally crossed the Indian Ocean. Greek and Roman writers had a great deal of respect for these trading partners who provided so many luxury goods for the people of the Mediterranean.

Egyptian soldiers from Hatshepsut's expedition to the Land of Punt as depicted from her temple at Deir el-Bahri. Photo by Σταύρος.

Why Don't We Know More About Ancient Africa?

Before you keep reading, ask someone you know how many civilizations they can name from ancient Africa. Or ask multiple people. Can they name any besides ancient Egypt? Some civilizations from the Middle Ages have become more famous recently. How many civilizations or empires can the same person or people name from Europe or Asia? There are many reasons why we know less about African history than about European or Asian history. Some are simple, and some are more complicated.

The Simple Reasons

- Archaeological conditions. In the damp jungle regions of Africa, wooden artifacts aren't likely to survive. Even bodies are more likely to decay. Desert regions, like those of Egypt, are much better for historical preservation. There is often more archaeological evidence from dry regions than from damp regions.

- Geography. There are many places on the continent of Africa that are not great places to live. These limited the spread of empires and meant many smaller cultural groups. Because there are so many smaller groups, there is not a single large civilization to study the way we look at the Roman Empire or ancient Greece.

- Because of the geographic limits on empires, these smaller groups could continue to rely on oral tradition rather than developing writing systems. Many ancient writing systems were born of bureaucracy. In other words, rulers needed writing to help manage empires that covered a lot of territory. So we don't have as many written primary sources from early African civilizations other than Egypt.

The Complicated Reasons

- Historians value written history over oral history. On the surface, that makes sense. Written history stays the same for thousands of years. Oral tradition does not provide precise dates. But historians are starting to place more value on oral tradition, acknowledging that both written and oral sources have their limitations. The preference for written over oral also comes from a European-centric study for history.

- People thought Africa wasn't worth studying. Until about 50 years ago, very few historians

62

put their energy towards African studies. A lot of this was because of racism by European and American scholars. While people have studied Egypt, Greece, and Rome for...well forever... in depth historical study of African cultures is relatively new. Historians also often generalized based on European impressions of African cultures. They decided that Africans were all polytheists, for example, because there were so many African gods. In truth, many of these cultures were monotheists. They just all had different single gods.

- Archaeologists still have a lot of exploring to do too. Just like historians haven't spent a lot of time studying the history of Africa through written and oral sources, there are many archaeological sites in Africa waiting to be explored and studied.

Does it matter what we study? Yes, absolutely. Understanding the history of the African continent helps us understand our world today. The map we look at today shows fifty-four countries. Yet the citizens of these countries are descended from many different cultural groups, and their ancestors did not draw these borders. African borders, for the most part, were drawn by Europeans. Yet, Africans are connected deeply to their ancient ancestors. The Somali language is in the same language family as ancient Egyptian, and modern Somali people still name their children after ancient Egyptian gods. The modern people of Ghana and Mali named their countries after medieval empires. If you want to learn more about ancient African civilizations, look up the Kingdom of Axum; Carthage; and the Nok Culture.

Camels

When you think of animals that live in a desert, chances are you think of camels. There are two main kinds of camels: bactrian and dromedary. Bactrian camels have two humps and dromedary camels have just one. Worried about remembering that one? Just keep in mind that the humps of a Bactrian camel look like a B and the hump of a Dromedary looks like a D. Most of the world's camels are dromedary camels, and the world's largest population of camels live in modern-day Somalia. No one knows exactly when or where the first camels were domesticated, but Somalia is in the front running. Dromedary camels were domesticated in Somalia about 3000 BC/BCE. Camels were game changers when it came to desert trade.

Camels are well adapted to life in a desert. Their broad, two-toed hooves help support them on shifting sand. Their famous humps help them survive too. The humps aren't actually full of water. Instead, they are full of fat. Because a camel's fat is concentrated in its hump, it doesn't make the body overheat. Then, when the camel burns the fat, it releases water into the respiratory system and is reabsorbed into the body. They can also withstand dehydration, drink large volumes of water in a very short period of time, and withstand incredible changes in body temperature. They have thick wool coats, which help insulate them against heat as well as cold. A shaved camel actually sweats more than a hairy one.

The Berbers of Africa saw the advantages of such a useful animal. They traveled in caravans of thousands of camels, bring goods across the Sahara and connecting northern Africa with sub-Saharan Africa. Camels were able to travel across the desert much faster than horses or donkeys. They are able to maintain a speed of 25 miles per hour over long distances and cover a greater distance in a day than other pack animals. The Berber's ability to navigate the desert using camels gave them a near monopoly on trans-Saharan trade.

FURTHER READING

All Ages
There are no books specifically about ancient Somalia written for children.

The Shipwrecked Sailor by Tamara Bower. The author and illustrator of this book is a professional archaeological illustrator specializing in ancient Egypt. She uses her skills in art history and hieroglyphics in this retelling of a story from the 19th century BC/BCE. Why include it here? This famous story is about a shipwrecked sailor who landed in Punt, and the ships are based on the ones that Queen Hatshepsut sent to Punt during her reign.

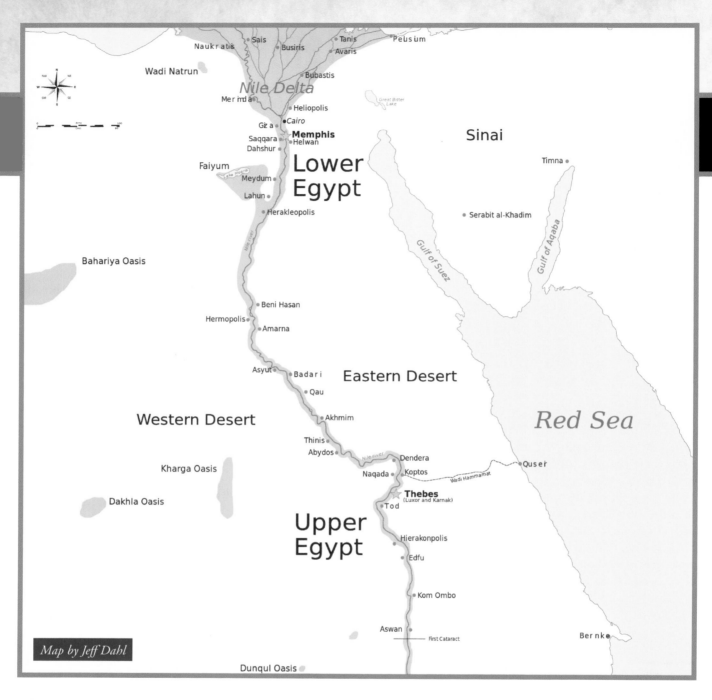

Map by Jeff Dahl

The reign of Akhenaten was possibly the most unique reign in all of Egyptian history. Religious beliefs, cultural practices, and even art underwent enormous changes during this time. After Akhenaten's rule ended, Egypt largely went back to the way things had been before.

Akhenaten was born Amenophis IV, the tenth pharaoh of the 18th Dynasty. He changed his name to Akhenaten after his ascent to the throne, to honor the rule of the god Aten. When Akhenaten first took power, he elevated the sun god, Amun Re, to the position of supreme deity. However, the pharaoh soon

began insisting that Amun Re was actually Aten, the one god. Akhenaten, as the son of Aten, was the only human intermediary. For the first time in Egyptian history, a god was represented not as a human or as a human/animal hybrid, but as a symbol: a disc representing the sun. Along with this representation, Akhenaten ordered art to become more representative.

The new theology did nothing for Akhenaten's popularity. The priest class resented the pharaoh's dominance over the new religion, and his closure or takeover of temples dedicated to other gods. Akhenaten paid

PHARAOHS

more attention to his new religion than to his kingly duties, and the kingdom suffered as a result. Both military leaders and diplomatic officials became disgruntled. Others felt angry over the move of the capital from Thebes to the new city of Akhetaten.

After his death, a (most likely) female pharaoh ruled briefly, under the name of Smenkhkhare. Historians debate whether or not Smenkkhare was the name of one of Akhenaten's lesser wives, or another name for his queen, Nefertiti. Regardless, her short reign was succeeded by the reign of Tutankhaten[1], better known by the name he took upon his own ascension to the throne: Tutankhamun. Even the new name showed a rejection of the previous king's theology. Tutankhaten meant "Living Image of Aten" while Tutankhamun meant "Living Image of Amun" and showed a return to the previous theological dominance of Amun. The capital returned to its place in Thebes and Egyptians attempted to erase Akhenaten's reign from their history, referring to him only as the heretic king. Tutankhamun, the boy king, ruled for only ten years, before his mysterious death at the age of nineteen. Howard Carter's discovery of Tutankhamun's tomb in 1925 became one of the greatest archeological discoveries of all time, as the tomb had remained completely undisturbed for thousands of years. Tut's mask, in particular, is possibly the most famous Egyptian artifact. The tomb contained furniture, personal items, and artwork that gave incredible insight into the life of the pharaohs. Tut himself ruled for a short time and did little of influence as he ruled largely under the control of regents, but became renowned in modern times because of the richness of his tomb.

The pyramids were about a thousand years old during Akhenaten and Tutankhamun's lifetime, and another thousand years would pass before Alexander the Great's victories marked the beginning of the Greco-Roman period in Egyptian history.

Around the world at this time, the Urnfield culture, a bronze-age culture in central Europe, appeared. Assyria rose as an independent power in Mesopotamia. India and Asian civilizations had largely reached an iron age level of technology.

King Tutankhamun's mask, made of gold and inlaid glass and gemstones, was discovered in 1925 by Howard Carter. Photo by Roland Unger.

---

1. Tutankhamun may or may not be Akhenaten's son. DNA evidence proves that Tutankhamun is the son of a mummy in a tomb that most Egyptologists believe to be Akhenaten's. His mother was Akhenaten's wife and sister (not Nefertiti).

Hieroglyphics

From the 7th century BC/BCE until the 19th century, BC/BCE, Egyptian hieroglyphics were a mysterious and silent language. No one knew whether the writings of the ancient Egyptians were figurative, symbolic, or phonetic. Imagine having many artifacts covered in ancient Egyptian writing with no way to read what they said. Then, in one of history's most famous discoveries, in Rosetta, Egypt in 1799, a French soldier discovered a stone inscribed with three different languages: Ancient Greek, Demotic, and hieroglyphs. For the next several decades, scholars attempted to translate the hieroglyphs using the Greek inscription as a key. Finally, in 1822, the Frenchman Jean Francois Champollion broke the code and discovered that Egyptian hieroglyphs were "a complex system, a writing that is figurative, symbolic, and phonetic all within the same text, a single sentence, I would even say a single word." In other words, a hieroglyph of a duck can have three separate meanings. It can mean duck (figurative). When used next to a hieroglyph of the sun, it means "son" of the sun, or pharaoh (symbolic). It can also be pronounced "SA" (phonetic).

Rosetta Stone. Photo by Hans Hillewaer

FURTHER READING

All Ages
Tutankhamun by Demi. Readers of all ages will love the gilded illustrations done loosely in the style of ancient Egyptian art.

Ages 5-9
You are There! Ancient Egypt 1336 BC by Wendy and Blane Conklin. The book puts you in the shoes of the boy king himself, with a sense of humor. This will be a great read-aloud for the younger set.

Seeker of Knowledge: The Man Who Deciphered Egyptian Hieroglyphs by James Rumford. Champollion was fascinated by ancient Egypt from an early age and Egyptology became his lifelong passion. It's a great story about following your passions as well as the thrill of discovery.

Ages 10-15
The Pharaohs of Ancient Egypt by Elizabeth Payne. One chapter of this book provides an excellent account of Akhenaten's life, why his father began worship of Aten, and why the Egyptian people were angered by the changes to their religion. The book was originally published in 1964 and some of the genealogy has been contested since then. It's a great overview of Egyptian history written in an engaging style.

Nefertiti

In 1912, a German archaeological team discovered the Bust of Nefertiti. Archaeologists identified the sculpture as Nefertiti because of the iconic crown, described in writings about Akhenaten's queen. The limestone and stucco bust, carved by the sculptor Thutmose and found in his studio, has become one of the most iconic images of ancient Egypt and a symbol of feminine beauty. The bust shows elements both of the older Egyptian style and the new Amarna style developed under Akhenaten. In addition, the bust has remained in German possession since its discovery and has become an important symbol within German culture as well.

Bust of Nefertiti. Photo by Philip Pikart

Papyrus

The papyrus plant grew along the Nile River in Ancient Egypt and was used to make boats, sandals, mats, baskets, medicine, and even perfume. The most famous use of papyrus, however, was the thick paper that is made from the pith of the plant. The English word "paper" even comes from the word "papyrus." Books made of papyrus have been found in ancient Egypt, but they look more like scrolls than how you would picture a book. Most papyrus books were only a few feet long, but some were much longer... up to 150 feet! Both words and beautiful painted images have been discovered on papyrus artifacts giving us a look into the records and art of the ancient Egyptians.

Mediterranean Sea

ASHER

NAPHTALI
★ Cedes

★ Hazor

★ Kinneret

ZEBULUN
★ Acsaf
★ Helcat
Jocneam ★
Dor ★
Mount Tabor ▲
★ Cammat
★ Astarot

BASAN

★ Edrei

ISSACHAR
★ Jafia
★ Jezreel
★ Megiddo
★ Kamon

★ Ramot de Galaad

★ Taanach
★ Beit She'an

MANASSEH
★ Tirza
Samir ★
★ Siquem

★ Zafon
★ Mahanaim

MANASSEH

River Jordan

Piraton ★

Gat-Rimon
Jaffa
★ Afec
Silo ★

EPHRAIM
★ Betel
★ Ai

GAD
★ Jazer

AMON
★ Rabbath Amon

DAN
Elteke ★
Gezer ★
Bet-Horon ★
Gabaon ★
Gilgal ★
Gibeton ★
Ekron ★
BENJAMIN
★ Jerusalem
Jericho ★
★ Hesbon
★ Mefaat
★ Beser
Mount Nebo ▲

Ashdod ★

Ashkelon ★
★ Gat
Jarmut ★
★ Bethlehem

REUBEN
★ Jahaza

PHILISTIA
Gaza ★
Laquis ★

JUDAH
★ Hebron
Debir ★
★ Estemoa

Gerar ★

Beersheba ★
★ Arad

SIMEON

Dead Sea

MOAB
★ Kir-Hareset

AMALEC
Wilderness of Zin

Zoar ★

EDOM
Tamar ★ Zalmona ★
★ Bosra

Map by Richardprins.

Note: The Bible is one of the secondary source documents that we used to learn about this period. The Old Testament books covering this period were written several hundred years after King David's reign. Primary sources come from other cultures at the time, such as Egypt. These primary sources and archaeological evidence support some of the stories told in the Bible. A 8th or 9th century BC/BCE stele fragment from Tel Dan references "The House of David," and a much older stele from Egypt, the Merneptah Stele, tells of "Israel." The Merneptah stele dates from the 13th century BC/BCE, and is the oldest non-biblical reference to Israel. The Bible, the Qu'ran, and the Torah are all secondary sources that tell stories about the Israelites. For many Christians, Jews, and Muslims, these sacred texts tell important stories of their cultural history and are taken as fact. Others believe that the stories in these religious texts, while based on facts, were written centuries after the events they described and may not be entirely factual. Even today, historians disagree about what really happened, and many biblical scholars interpret the Bible differently, forming their own conclusions about the truth. Educators should provide the framework and interpretation that best fits the needs of their students.

ISRAELITES

Many students throughout the ages have wondered "why do we have to learn about this?" Sometimes, it's difficult to make a connection between historical events and the world today. However, in the case of the Israelites, their history has a direct impact on global politics today. World civilization began in the Middle East more than ten thousand years ago. About five thousand years later, around 3000 BC/BCE, people began settling the region of Canaan, an area along the eastern coast of the Mediterranean Sea. Three different civilizations developed in the area. The first were the Phoenicians, who lived along the coast and became navigators, sailors, and traders. The second were the "Hebrew People," later called the Israelites. They settled in the hills that would become Palestine. The Phoenicians and Israelites largely enjoyed a peaceful trade relationship. In fact, the Phoenician alphabet is the ancestor of the modern Hebrew alphabet. And finally, a group called the "Sea Peoples" came from Egypt and settled south of Palestine, along the coast of the Mediterranean. They became known as Philistines and often fought in wars against the Israelites.

When they first arrived in the region, the Israelites lived in small villages on sparsely settled hills. The terrain was not suited for agriculture, so they invented terraced farming. Terraced farming involves building stepped fields into hillsides supported with retaining walls. They grew a variety of crops, but wheat, barley, and olives were the primary crops. Wheat and barley were used for bread and beer, while olive trees provided shade, food, and oil used for cooking and lamps. Over time, the Israelites grew more prosperous and became a United Monarchy during the 11th century, possibly under King Saul. After his rule, King David reigned for about fifty years, followed by his son, Solomon. Under David and Solomon, the Israelites built several cities, including the capital, Jerusalem. They believed that God, or Yahweh, was present in Jerusalem. This made the city a holy land for the Israelites. The city was home to the Temple of Jerusalem, where religious festivals were celebrated with ceremonies that included animal sacrifice. According to historians, the Israelites may have worshipped other gods beside Yahweh until they became exiled as captives in Babylon in the sixth century BC/BCE. At that time, the religion became monotheistic.

Although Israel, the kingdom of the Israelites, had prosperous trade relationships with allies such as the Phoenician kingdom of Tyre, it also became embroiled in conflict with other Mediterranean neighbors. Over the centuries, Israel fought with the Philistines, Assyria, Egypt, and Babylon. These conflicts over the rights to the land are echoes of modern conflicts in the region. Today, two modern peoples, the Palestinians and the Israelis, both claim rights to the area surrounding Jerusalem. As the birthplace of Judaism, the city is also the ancestral home of the two other Abrahamic religions: Christianity and Islam. Adherents of all three religions believe that they are the religious descendents of a shepherd named Abram, a man who came to Canaan from the Sumerian city of Ur in Mesopotamia. Because members of all three religions believe Jerusalem is their sacred city, it has been a center of conflict from as far back as the Crusades and into modern times. This makes the history of the Israelites relevant even today.

Have you ever heard of an underdog winning a competition described as David defeating Goliath? Or maybe you've heard of the Wisdom of Solomon? Several of the stories about the kings of the Israelites from ancient history are still commonly told and referenced today.

David and Goliath

At the time when Saul was king of Israel, there was a war with the neighboring nation of the Philistines. Among the Philistine warriors was a giant of a man—he towered above the other soldiers on the battlefield. His armor was bronze scale and glittered in the sunlight, and he carried a spear with a shaft as thick as a man's arm and a spearhead that weighed as much as a child! Every day he would walk to the front lines and shout his challenge: "This day I defy the armies of Israel! Give me a man and let us fight each other. If I win, you must be our servants. But if your man wins, we will serve you and your king!"

When the Israelites saw Goliath, they were afraid. Who could face him in one-on-one combat? Not one man wanted to step forward and fight the giant. Day after day, the challenge was unmet and the spirits of the Israelite army sank lower and lower.

painting by Robert Temple Ayres

Among the men in the army were three brothers: Eliab, Abinadab, and Shammah. They had followed King Saul to war, but they, too, were afraid to face Goliath. They hid in the camp of the Israelites with the other soldiers, wondering what to do next. It was at that time that their youngest brother, David, who had been too young to follow them to war, came to bring food and drink to replenish their supplies. When he heard about Goliath he asked, "Who is this Philistine, that he should defy the army of the living God?"

Eliab replied, "Why have you come here? You should be back tending the sheep! You know nothing of battle."

But David would not leave and would not be silent. Soon he was summoned by the King. David said to Saul, "Let no one lose heart on account of this Philistine; I will go and fight him."

The king protested. "You cannot win against him. He is a seasoned warrior and you are only a boy!"

David replied, "For years I have been tending my father's sheep. Once a lion attacked, and another time, it was a bear. When these beasts tried to carry off my father's sheep I went after them. I struck them down and rescued the sheep. This Philistine will be like one of them. The Lord who rescued me from the paw of the lion and the paw of the bear will rescue me from the hand of this Philistine."

Saul said to David, "Go, and the Lord be with you."

Saul gave David his finest weapons and dressed him in the best armor. But when David tried to walk, he found that he could not bear so much weight, so he took them off. Then he took his shepherd's staff in his hand, chose five smooth stones from the stream, put them in the pouch of his shepherd's bag, and, with his sling in his hand, approached the Philistine.

When Goliath saw that David was no more than a boy, he was insulted. He said to David, "Am I a dog, that you come at me with sticks?"

David replied, "You come against me with sword and spear and javelin, but I come against you in the name of the Lord Almighty, the God of the armies of Israel. All those gathered here will know that it is not by sword or spear that the Lord saves; for the battle is the Lord's, and he will give all of you into our hands."

As the Philistine moved closer to attack him, David ran quickly toward the battle line to meet him. Reaching into his bag and taking out a stone, he slung it and struck the Philistine on the forehead. The stone sank into his forehead, and he fell face down on the ground. So David triumphed over the Philistine with a sling and a stone; without a sword in his hand he struck down Goliath and killed him.

Solomon's Judgment

King Solomon was revered by the Israelites as one of the wisest men that ever lived. There are several famous stories about his judgment, and how he used it to solve seemly unsolvable problems. The following is a retelling of the most famous example.

Two women who lived together came before Solomon with a baby boy. Both women told him the same story. "This is my son! That woman, whom I live with, is trying to steal him from me. She had a baby boy the same age but, sadly, he died in the night. Now she is grief stricken and claiming that my baby is hers. Tell her that the baby is mine and she must give him to me!"

Solomon considered the women and pondered. There was no evidence or witnesses. Nothing except the word of one woman against the other. How could he ensure that the child went with the right woman? After a moment, he pronounced his judgment. "There is one child and two mothers. What can be done? We must divide the remaining child in half, and give half to each."

Upon hearing the terrible verdict the first woman shouted "If he cannot be mine, than he will be no one's. Divide him!" But the second woman fell at Solomon's feet and begged "Do not harm him, my lord! Give him to the other woman if you must, only let him live!"

Then Solomon knew who the baby's true mother was. The child was sent home with the woman who had asked for mercy, who was willing to give up her child in order to save his life.

Cheese of the Herd

Why raise animals for dairy? If you raise up a cow, a sheep, or a goat for slaughter, it only provides food one time. However, if you raise up one of these same animals for dairy, they can provide food daily for long periods of time. Given this logic, it becomes clear why the Israelites only consumed meat on special occasions. But in a hot, desert environment, without modern refrigeration, milk doesn't last very long. Cheese, on the other hand, is a lot more stable. No one knows exactly who invented cheese, but it happened sometime about 4,000 years ago. One ancient legend credits an Arab trader who stored milk in a sheep's stomach before setting off across the desert for his journey. The lining of the stomach contains rennet, an enzyme complex used to coagulate milk (separate milk into curds and whey) in cheesemaking. Between the rennet and the hot desert temperatures, the Arab trader discovered that his milk had turned into curds and whey by nightfall.

No matter who invented cheese, or how it happened, the Israelites definitely consumed cheese. Cheese is even mentioned in early texts such as the Talmud and Bible.

"Now when David had come to Mahanaim, Shobi the son of Nahash from Rabbah of the sons of Ammon, Machir the son of Ammiel from Lo-debar, and Barzillai the Gileadite from Rogelim, brought beds, basins, pottery, wheat, barley, flour, parched grain, beans, lentils, parched seeds, honey, curds, sheep, and cheese of the herd, for David and for the people who were with him, to eat; for they said, "The people are hungry and weary and thirsty in the wilderness.""

-2 Samuel 17:27-29

The Olive Tree

To discover the importance of the olive tree in ancient times, one need only look at ancient writings and legends. The Bible is filled with examples of the uses of olive oil and metaphors about olive trees. The Greek legend about the founding of Athens revolves around the gifts provided by an olive tree. Why was this little tree so important to ancient peoples?

The olive tree grows in inhospitable conditions: dry, rocky soil under a hot sun. The tree is evergreen and extremely long-lived. In Croatia, there is a 1,600 year-old olive tree that still produces oil-laden fruit. There are olive trees that some claim to be as old as 4,000 years old! The ancient Israelites ate the fruit (the olive) and used the oil for light, cooking, and ritual anointing. The wood is very hard, and was useful for making kitchen utensils and bowls.

Make A Joyous Noise

Through the Bible and through archaeological evidence, we know that music was an important part of daily life for the Israelites. They sang songs while they worked to make their tasks less arduous. They sang to mark major life events. They sang and played instruments as part of religious rites. And sometimes, they sang just for joy. Gatherings such as harvest festivals or shearing provided opportunities for music and dance. Aside from the universal musical instrument of the human voice, the Israelites used the shofar (a horn made from a ram's horn), the timbrel (tambourine), and the goblet drum. They also had a variety of stringed instruments, mostly variations on the lyre, such as the the nevel (psaltery), the kithara, and the kinnor. In the Bible, King David is described as playing the nevel and the kinnor. These stringed instruments would have been used both secularly and religiously, either for vocal accompaniment or for dancing.

FURTHER READING

All Ages
Bible Lands by Jonathan N. Tubb. Another one of the DK Eyewitness books, this one covers the Canaanites, the Israelites, and the Phoenicians. This book provides context for the history as well as photographs of historical artifacts and a section on using the Bible as evidence. Out of print, so check your local library and used book sites.

Ages 5-9
Ancient Israelites and Their Neighbors: An Activity Guide (Cultures of the Ancient World) by Marian Broida. As with any book about the Israelites, this book uses the Bible as a secondary source document but also discusses archaeological evidence and other sources with equal weight. It is a secular book with hands on activities to help kids connect, along with plenty of historical information. It is clear about which information comes from the Bible and which comes from other sources.

Ages 10-15
The Israelites: The Children of Israel by Katherine Reece. While written from a secular perspective, this book uses the Bible as a major source of information. The sections on daily life are particularly interesting. The book also provides information about Israel today. Out of print, so check your local library and used book sites.

Portion of the Temple Scroll, labeled 11Q19, one of the longest of the Dead Sea Scrolls. Source: he Israel Museum's 'Dead Sea Scrolls Digital Project

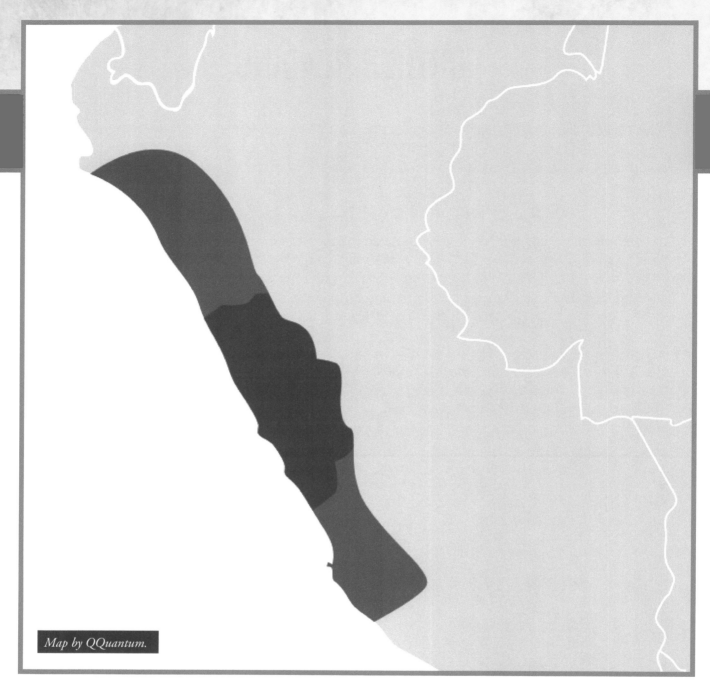

In the Andean highlands of Peru stand the ruined monuments of an ancient civilization. They had no written language and we do not know what they called themselves. According to local oral history, the name of the site, Chavín de Huantar, comes from a Quechua word meaning "center." Today, we call the long-lost civilization the Chavin after this site. The building of this complex began around 900 BC/BCE and the civilization had faded by around 200 BC/BCE.

At first, the Chavín had two small settlements near the larger site, where several hundred people lived. They hunted deer and llamas, collected clams and other shellfish, and hunted guinea pigs and birds. They also grew maize and potatoes, although potatoes were the crop best suited for the highland climate. As time went on, people moved closer to the culture's center at Chavín de Huantar. They domesticated the llama to use as a pack animal as well as for its meat and fiber. They gradually stopped hunting deer. They started interacting with other civilizations in the area and using more ceramics. Ceramics are objects shaped from clay and hardened from heating in a fire. While they had used ceramics

CHAVIN CULTURE

(pots and other objects made of heated clay) from the beginning, ceramic production became more centralized and common. By the end of their time, they were beginning to develop into a more urban culture with distinct social classes and a more dense population. No one knows exactly why they faded away.

Be an Anthropologist

Imagine that you are visiting the Chavín de Huantar site. You are in the lush green mountains of the Andes in Peru, facing ancient buildings made of stacked stone. With your training, you can imagine how it once looked: a sunken plaza surrounded by huge structures up on platforms. As you walk around, you write down your observations.

- The buildings are made of quartzite, white granite, and black limestone. These materials were brought from far off places, either by workers or through trade.
- Under one of the buildings are canals that carry flood waters during the rainy season. The rushing water makes the roaring sound of a jaguar. The jaguar is one of the sacred animals of this culture. The canals could also have been used to make fountains at the surface using natural water pressure.
- Long galleries, or passages, twist and turn deep into the mounds of earth at the site. They are windowless and filled with sharp turns, dead ends, and changes in floor height.
- Elaborate carvings decorate gateways.
- Scattered human and llama bones that have been broken, burned, or marked with cuts.

- There are deposits of broken pottery that was new when it was broken and was broken deliberately.
- One gallery contained *pututus,* or horns made of conch shells. They had once been carefully wrapped in fabric, now decayed. Ducts from this gallery would have carried the sound of the *pututus* to people in the plaza outside.
- Many elements often found in ancient villages are missing from this site.
  - No hearths suitable for cooking.
  - No midden, or trash, deposits.
  - No obvious storage for every day goods like food.
  - No defensive structures and few weapons.
  - No complete burials.

Based on this evidence, can you make a hypothesis about the purpose of this site? Do you think it was a residential or ritual space?

Anthropologists believe that this site was primarily used for religious ceremonies. Any debris was probably cleared away after ceremonies. Priests may have used the site to emphasize their own power through the mysterious atmosphere of the galleries and the apparent magic of the *pututu* music and jaguar roars. The pottery was likely broken as part of a ritual sacrifice and created for that purpose. The buildings, generally called temples by anthropologists, probably served a special purpose based on the materials used to build them. The canals point to a culture that saw water as sacred.

Fun archaeological fact: The 3,000 year old *pututus* are in such good condition that they can still be played, allowing anthropologists to recreate the sacred sounds of a long-gone civilization.

Chavin Art

Stone

Carved stone is everywhere at Chavín. Stone carvings depict jaguars, snakes, alligators, and birds of prey. The Tello Obelisk (a tall pillar with a pyramid shape at the top, like the Washington Monument) was named for a scholar who studied this particular stone. It depicts something that looks like a dragon. The Lanzon giant, a nearly 15 feet shaft of granite carved to look like a fanged god, is depicted on modern Peruvian currency. It was probably the central deity based on its location in the oldest temple in the complex.

Gold

The Chavin were goldsmiths too. They used gold to make jewelry and other decorative objects. They may have even been the first people in South America to work with gold. One artifact is something called a pectoral, a flattened sheet of gold worn over the chest during ceremonial occasions. The goldsmith started by hammering a sheet of copper and gold alloy until it was flat. Then they used a sharp tool to carve the design, and hammered the sheet over a wooden mold to create a relief. Like the pottery, this work of art was then ritually damaged.

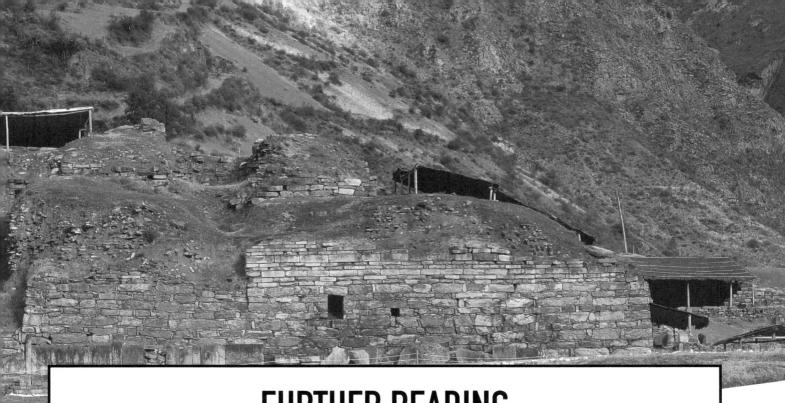

FURTHER READING

All Ages
There are no children's books specifically about the Chavin Culture but you may find tidbits by reading other children's history books about Peru.

Looking Back: Civilizations of Peru before 1535 by Hazel Mary Martell. There are only three pages about the Chavin, but there are also sections about other ancient and medieval Peruvian cultures from the Nazca to the Inca.

Pututus

While archaeology is our best tool for learning about the people of the past, sometimes it can be a delicate balance with showing respect for the living. The original residents of Chavin are long gone, but their indigenous descendants still live nearby. Each year, the excavation teams begin the season with a ceremony called a *pagapu*. During the *pagapu*, they make offerings to mountain spirits called *apus* to ask for a safe excavation season. There are speeches in Quechua, Spanish, and English. Then the people make their offerings. Instead of broken pottery and llama bones, they offer coca, candy, rum, and cigarettes. The ceremony concludes with the playing of the *pututu*. The music resonates through the jungle and bounces off the temples, and witnesses say its a haunting sound. Only when the music has faded can the archaeological work begin.

With the rediscovery of the *pututu,* indigenous Peruvians have connected with their own heritage. During the Spanish colonial era, the shells were largely replaced with cow horns but they never went away completely. They play *pututus* during their Independence Day marches, use traditional techniques to decorate them, and bring them to political events. When the first indigenous Peruvian president, Alejandro Toledo, was elected, the *pututu* was played at his inauguration.

Black Sea

HITTITE
EMPIRE

Sardes

Mycenae

CILICIA

ASSYRIA

Carchemish

Nineveh

SYRIA

Assur

MESOPOTAMIA

Citium

Byblos

Kadesh

Mediteranean Sea

Sidon

Tyre

Damascus

Babylon

Nippur

Gaza

Tanis

CANAAN

Ur

Avaris

SINAI

Memphis

Heliopolis

Persian
Gulf

LIBYA

Nile

Herakleopolis

ARABIA

EGYPTIAN

Abydos

THEBES

Red Sea

Aswan

Elephantine
I

Abu Simbel

II

EMPIRE

III

KUSH

IV

V

Napata

VI

PUNT
(under Egyptian influence)

Map by Andrei Nacu.

Around the time that the Great Pyramid of Giza was built by Egyptian pharaohs, a new kingdom was coming into power in the south. The Egyptians called the land "Ta-Seti", or "Land of the Bow" because it was home to famous archers. Later Greeks called them "Ethiopians" from a word which meant "burnt skin," referring to the darker skin of the people who lived there. Eventually, a Greek geographer named Strabo called them "Nubians" after the Noba tribe who lived there.

Located in modern day Sudan, the Nubian city of Kerma was rich and powerful. Kerma grew so powerful

that it became a threat to Egypt, and the pharaoh Thutmose I led an army to defeat the Kerma people. From the very beginning, Egyptian culture became intertwined with the culture of its neighbors to the south. The Greek historian Herodotus believed that the Nubians were the source of many Egyptian beliefs and practices. It's difficult to say who came first, but they shared many religious beliefs and traditions with each other. The Pharaohs took Nubian women into their harems, and intermarriage was common between Egyptians and Nubians. It was not just a one way

THE KINGDOM OF KUSH

power trip either. Eventually, the Nubian Kingdom of Kush turned the tables, winning back their homes and eventually taking over Egypt. They established the 25th dynasty of Egypt, ruling from the city of Napata and burying their kings in tombs in Kush. While their dynasty only lasted about a century before war with the Assyrians drove them south, the Kushites outlasted the pharaohs of Egypt. They moved the capital to Meroe and ruled until around 350 AD/CE, long after the Roman Empire took over Egypt. During their time at Meroe, they continued to trade with the people of the Mediterranean. The Greeks wanted elephants to rival the Asian elephants used by the armies of India, and formed elephant hunting expeditions with the help of the Nubian Kushites.

Most of what we know about the Kingdom of Egypt comes from writing in Egyptian or Greek. The Nubians had their own writing system, Meroitic. It was widely used, and based on 23 hieroglyphic signs. It had a cursive form as well, used for record keeping. Unfortunately, while historians know which characters represent which phonetic sounds, no one has been able to translate the language itself because it does not seem to be related to any other known languages. We are left to do our best with other sources and the archaeological evidence.

Were the Ancients Racist?

This is an excellent question. Without a doubt, ancient cultures felt prejudiced against other ancient cultures. The Greeks, in particular, demonstrated an attitude of general superiority over other cultures. They never hesitated to call others out as barbarians if their ways

were different. Yet, their judgement was not based on our modern ideas of race. The Greeks believed that the most savage of all races were the Irish, followed by the rest of the inhabitants of the British Isles. The Greeks blamed their savage ways on the extreme climate. Since they had the perfect culture, living in the mild climate of the Mediterranean, they assumed that extreme hot or cold temperatures led to barbaric behavior. Yet, it had nothing to do with color. Neither the Greeks or Romans showed prejudice based on color alone. Free or slave status mattered, but neither freedom nor slavery were based on skin color. Slaves were sometimes captured

Statue of the Kushite pharaoh Aspelta, Napata period (c. 620–580 BC). Photo by Keith Schengili-Roberts.

Meroitic prince smiting his enemies (early first century AD).

from other lands. Other times, people sold themselves or their children into slavery because of extreme poverty. Aristotle believed that anyone who wasn't Greek was more suited to slavery because non-Greeks were more willing to submit to authority.

It's possible that one of these slaves came from Nubia and rose to become a famous Greek storyteller. The Greeks called dark-skinned Africans "Aethiop" or "burnt-faced people," giving us the modern word Ethiopian. Some scholars think Aesop, of Aesop's fables, got his name from this word. Some ancient descriptions of Aesop fit this description as well. Many of his stories include animals like elephants, lions, crocodiles, primates, and camels. These animals are found in Nubia, but not in Greece. Nubian artifacts from the time depict many of these animals. There is also a long tradition of animal folklore in African storytelling tradition. Aesop told stories about Egypt, Ethiopians, and

the Nile. We know that Aesop was a slave in Greece, captured from another land, and that he eventually traveled to Egypt (or returned to Egypt). His stories became famous throughout the Greek world, and today we think of him as Greek. Is it possible that he was really Nubian?

So were ancient people racist? While the people of the ancient world showed prejudice against people who were different, the most important differences had nothing to do with skin color. Historic evidence indicates that racism, or the prejudice against another group based on skin color, did not yet exist. Skin color was just another physical trait.

The Pyramids of Kush

Ancient Egypt is famous for its pyramids, but in many ways, the pyramids built just up the Nile are even more impressive. The ancient Egyptians spent hundreds of years building about 120 pyramids. While they are larger than their southern counterparts, the Nubians built over 350 pyramids over a span of thousands of years. The last one was built at the very end, in 350 AD/CE. They are steeper than Egyptian pyramids, and built much closer together. For years, tomb robbers and archaeologists could not find a way into the burial chambers of these pyramids. In the 1830s, a doctor named Giuseppe Ferlini took up treasure hunting as a hobby and started the idea of blowing the tops of off tombs to find treasure. While he succeeded in getting to the burial chambers, he destroyed countless treasures in the process. Unfortunately, Ferlini had not figured out the big difference in construction between Egyptian and Nubian pyramids. In ancient Egypt, the pyramids themselves were tombs, with the burial chamber at the center of the pyramid. In Nubia, the burial chamber was underground. The funeral took place, the passage was filled in, and the pyramid was built on top of the burial site by the king's successor. In these burials, the kings mixed together Egyptian burial goods with Nubian traditions, such as the body being placed on a platform. Many of the tombs had archery artifacts, and all showed evidence of trade with the Greeks.

Pyramids of Nuri, built between the reigns of Taharqa and Nastasen. Photo by Bertramz.

FURTHER READING

Ages 5-9
Step Back in Time to Ancient Kush (Activity Book) by K.N. Chimbiri. Learn about the deities, clothing, rulers, and cities of Kush while completing puzzles and coloring pictures.

Ancient Egyptians and their Neighbors by Marian Broida. While the title is all Egyptian, there is a substantial chapter about Nubians with information about politics and daily life, along with hands on activities. It also covers Hittites and Mesopotamians.

Ages 10-15
Ancient Africa: Archaeology Unlocks the Secrets of Africa's Past by Victoria Sherrow. Chapter three covers Nubia, while the other chapters cover African cultures from human origins through the Middle Ages.

The Greek historian Herodotus wrote about the Scythians in the fifth century BC/BCE, and provided much of the information we have today. Unfortunately, he wrote about the Scythians in comparison to Greek and Egyptian culture, which he considered much more advanced, so some of his writings tend towards a biased portrayal of the Scythians as barbarians.

The Scythians spoke an early Indo-European language with no written form. However,they did have great skill in gold and bead work. The Scythians may have been among the earliest cultures to domesticate horses, which held a central role in the society. Scythians rode horses into battle and buried horses with their riders; both horse and rider decked out in fabulously decorated clothing. Scythians consumed horse meat and made cheese with horse milk. Many historians also credit these nomadic riders with the invention of pants,

much better suited for horseback riding than the tunics seen elsewhere in the ancient world.

The Scythians were also great archers. On horseback, with a bow and arrows, a woman could be an equal warrior to a man, and many women did become warriors. Around one third of women found in burial mounds were buried with weapons or showed evidence of war injuries. Women may also have been warriors because the tribes were small and every warrior was necessary. Scythian women may be the origin of the Greek legends of Amazon warrior women. Unlike the Amazons of legend, they did not reject men but fought alongside them. This idea may come from the tradition of fostering sons out to other tribes, a practice that built alliances between tribes and helped to keep the peace. Scythians wore clothing made of wool, hemp, wool felt, and leather, all suitable for the cold climate in which they lived (with temperatures often below freezing).

THE SCYTHIANS

One woman was found buried in a silk skirt, most likely due to trade with China. They may also have had linen clothing through their trade with Greece. The Scythians wore skillfully crafted gold jewelry as well, often with elaborate bead work of amber and turquoise. In addition to jewelry, they decorated their bodies with swirling blue tattoos of animals, both real and imaginary, particularly on their arms.

Because of the lack of a written Scythian language, our knowledge of their culture comes from accounts from people like Herodotus and from the artifacts in burial mounds. The culture included many tribes across a wide area, meaning that historians are faced with a great deal of contradictory or missing information. For example, we do not know for sure what the houses looked like, although we can conclude that they may have been similar to the yurts still used in the region today. In general, it seems that the Scythians were a nomadic people and yet there are some historians who say that they grew wheat. In addition, the Greek legends of Amazons both help guide historians and confuse the picture.

Around the world during this period (500-300 BC/BCE), many great changes were taking place. Gautama Buddha founded the Buddhist religion in the sixth century BC, at the same time that Confucius was teaching the Chinese people. Greek philosophy began its golden age with Socrates and Plato. At the very end of this period, construction began on what would become the world's largest pyramid: the Great Pyramid of Cholula in Mexico.

Eugène Delacroix's painting of the Roman poet, Ovid, in exile among the Scythians.

Scythian Horses

The ancient Greeks told stories of a mythical people: half human, half horse. These centaurs were generally depicted as wild and lawless. Today, historians believe that the Scythians were the possible inspiration for these myths. To the Greeks in their city-states, the fierce and nomadic Scythian tribes were terrifying barbarians. One thing that made the Scythians such formidable foes was their skill on horseback.

The Scythians were among the earliest riders in Central Asia, and their skill on horseback was incredible. They trained their horses for battle, teaching them to bite and kick in a fight, as well as kneel to allow a wounded warrior to mount from the ground. They used bridles with bits to control the horse, but rode without stirrups, on top of saddle cloths made of wool felt and leather. Their knees provided most of the control, leaving their hands free to fire arrows from horseback. The Scythians invented pants to facilitate riding. As a nomadic tribe, most of the tribe would have spent a great deal of time in the saddle. Even the skeleton of a thirteen or fourteen year old girl already showed bowing of the leg bones indicating extensive time on horseback. The horses allowed the Scythians to move quickly in both peace and wartime, making them difficult to find or attack. When they were traveling on horseback, they were able to spend days in the saddle subsisting on mare's cheese and licorice root. The cheese provided needed calories, while chewing the licorice root (known as Scythian root to the Greeks) helped stave off dehydration.

Horses were central to Scythian culture, as shown in the extensive representation of horses in Scythian artwork. The Siberian Ice Maiden, as one Scythian mummy is known, wore a wig of horsehair and bore tattoos of horses on her skin. Horses were valued not only as mounts for war and travel, but as beasts of burden and providers of meat and dairy. The Scythians used mare's milk to make butter, cheese, and the fermented drink known today as koumiss. These valuable animals have frequently been found in burial sites, sacrificed to travel along with their owners to the underworld. Most of these sacrificed horses were older, around twenty years old. One horse shows evidence of being lame, meaning that his owner kept him and cared for him out of affection, rather than utility. For the Scythians, wealth was measured in horses, and one wealthy warrior was buried with four hundred horses. These sacrificed horses were decked out in gold pendants, garlands, ornaments, and gold-bedecked saddle cloths.

Thanks to these burial sites, we have a pretty good idea of what the horses looked like. Some were preserved with their skin and hair intact. For mounts, the Scythians preferred reddish brown horses such as chestnuts or bays. It's possible that this reflects a practice of sun worship. They also rejected any horse with white

Battle between the Scythians and the Slavs (Viktor Vasnetsov, 1881).

markings, which fits with a modern idea that horses with white fetlocks (the hair around the horse's ankle) have weaker hooves. In rough terrain, without horseshoes, Scythian horses had to have tough feet and be sure-footed. They were also small horses by today's standards. They were between 58 and 59 inches tall, which puts them just slightly taller than the modern size classification of a pony. However, for the time period, they would have been considered large horses. There were three distinct breeds, all fairly similar to today's Altai Horse which lives in Siberia. They rode both stallions and mares into battle, stallions being favored for their spirit and mares being practical for their ability to continue galloping even while urinating. The Scythian rider would have been a spectacular sight, moving as one with a well-dressed horse. Saddle cloths were often painted, embroidered or appliqued and wealthy riders used bridles and reins covered in gold. The highest ranking Scythians also used gold on their saddle cloths during life and when they were buried. Throughout life and into death, the horse was a central part of Scythian life.

A Pazyryk horseman in a felt painting from a burial around 300 BC. The Pazyryks appear to be closely related to the Scythians.

FURTHER READING

All Ages
There aren't many books about the Scythians for young learners. Look for general books about ancient civilizations to find more tidbits.

The Griffin and the Dinosaur by Marc Aronson with Adrienne Mayor. Ancient people told stories about cyclops, centaurs, and griffins. But where did they get the ideas? Adrienne Mayor believes they found fossils from mammoths, dinosaurs, and other extinct creatures. The Scythians told stories of griffins guarding gold deposits. Mayor decided to find out the true origins of the griffin. Great for history buffs and dinosaur lovers alike, and the best pick for our younger historians.

Scythians and Sarmations by Kathryn Hinds. Although this book is part of a series about barbarians, the introduction explains the term and that the perception of people, like the Scythians, as "wild, uncivilized, and uncultured" comes from historians like Herodotus and Tacitus (Greek and Roman), who provide much of the story. This book draws information from nearby historians, but also from artifacts found in the kurgans. This book also places the Scythians in a greater historical context. This book is out of print, but worth tracking down. It's a recommended book by Adrienne Mayor.

The Ancient Horsemen of Siberia by Janet Buell
I love this book because it weaves together the story of the Scythians with the excitement of the archaeologists who excavated the kurgans and the emotions of the people who still lived in the area. Out of print, so check those libraries and used book sites.

The Problem With Looters

When archaeologists began excavating Sengileevskoe 2, a Scythian kurgan, they did not believe they would have any luck. They had already found evidence of looters beating them to the dig, likely hundreds of years before the archaeologists arrived. But, they lucked out: a thick layer of clay covered a stone-lined lower chamber containing gold cups, gold buckets, and gold jewelry. The discovery was a wonderful surprise. The looting, however, was anything but surprising. Around thirty monumental kurgans have been discovered, and only one was free from looting. This particular burial complex was a spectacular find, showing no evidence of looting

and rich with treasure and information about Scythian culture. It's possible that the Scythians themselves took measures to protect these tombs from looters: traditionally the kings were buried in the center of kurgans, so looters usually dug straight down into the center to find the richest goods. In this particular complex, several of the burials were offset from the center. Instead, would-be looters discovered only empty pits at the center of the kurgans. Aside from the loss of treasure, looting causes damage to artifacts and removes context. One of the oldest known Scythian burial sites, dating back to the 9th or 8th century BC/BCE, had just enough left to determine that it was likely a royal burial complex, but so much had been taken that it was impossible to determine much more than that.

Looting is certainly not a unique problem for historians of this era. Illegal antiquities trading dates back thousands of years. In New York City, there is a secret warehouse that provides permanent or temporary

storage for illegally traded artifacts. Right now, they have an enormous stone Buddha from India, terracotta horsemen from China, and an Egyptian sarcophagus and mummy. The mummy, a woman named Shesepamuntayesher, was removed from her coffins, and her sarcophagus was sawed into four pieces to be mailed across the ocean from Egypt to the United States, where she and her possessions were eventually discovered by US Customs agents. A June 2016 National Geographic article neatly sums up why these thefts are so tragic, even if the artifacts are eventually recovered (which often does not happen). "Shesepamuntayesher is valuable because of her hieroglyphs and paintings, but properly excavated she'd be priceless--the difference between a page torn from a book and an entire book, set in a large library." Without context, we lose a lot of information about how artifacts fit into history. On top of that, looters typically destroy hundreds of objects for every object they remove. They take only what looks valuable and in sellable condition, and generally leave everything else in a jumble. In Egypt, at least a quarter of known archaeological sites have major damage from looting. Additionally, proper excavation takes into account environmental conditions that can endanger artifacts. In Scythian burials, permafrost conditions, clay, and copper salt residues from bronze artifacts have helped preserve organic materials like leather, felt, and wood. In the case of a large cache of sacrificed horses, archaeologists dug up entire icy blocks of earth to be removed to cold labs for study, so that they would not decay too quickly. Looters take no such care.

Looting tends to be a problem in areas where people are struggling economically, although it can happen anywhere. Some of the earliest looting in Egypt took place about 3,000 years ago. The tombs of Ramses V and Ramses VI in the Valley of the Kings were both looted. It was a period of economic crisis and foreign invasion. Likewise, looting of Egyptian archaeological sites increased dramatically after the Egyptian revolution in 2011 as unemployment skyrocketed. In Cambodia, looting thrived under the Khmer Rouge during the Cambodian revolution, from the 1970s onward.

While many of these artifacts end up in private collections, never to be seen again, others end up in museum collections or special exhibitions on loans from private individuals. In theory, these artifacts must be obtained legally and the owner must know the origins of the object. However, the rules are not strictly followed, and origins are not always clear. This has led to many ethical debates about the antiquities trade. Museums provide education as well as proper care for the collections. Is it better for a museum to own an object obtained illegally than for an artifact to be returned to its country of origin if that country is unstable? Museums in Iraq and Egypt have been raided and damaged, with an incredible loss of priceless artifacts. Some argue that the artifacts belong to those countries, no matter the danger, while others argue that the priority should be protection. What do you think?

Looting of archaeological sites does not only occur in Africa or the Middle East. It is a problem all over the world, and you can help. An Egyptologist named Sarah Parcack has developed a website to catch looters. Currently, volunteers can look at sites in Peru to find evidence of tampering and looting.

Visit http://www.nationalgeographic.org/projects/space-archaeology/ to find out more.

Scythians And Their Gold

For historians, burial sites are often rich sources of information about people who lived long ago. For the Scythians, who left behind no written record of their own, burial sites are both rich in the sense of information and in the monetary value of their contents. One burial site, consisting of more than two dozen kurgans, or burial mounds, held thousands of gold objects as well as providing insights into the traditions of the Scythian upper class.

The majority of the written history of the Scythians comes from the ancient Greek historian Herodotus. Given that he generally regarded the Scythians as barbaric nomadic warriors, his writing was not exactly free from bias. However, the archaeological evidence seems to confirm at least some of what he wrote. His history tells the following story: "In the open space around the body of the king they bury one of his concubines and also his cup-bearer, his cook, his groom, his lackey, his messenger, some of his horses... and some golden cups, for they use neither silver nor brass." In the grave site mentioned above, known as Arzhan 2, the bodies of a royal man and woman were found in one mound, arranged side by side. Both had been adorned with at least a pound's worth of gold in the form of jewelry and beaded clothing. They were clearly both of high status. The surrounding graves held bodies that had also been dressed in gold jewelry.

Another grave site gives a glimpse into the stories that were important to the Scythians. One kurgan held two bowl-like vessels with elaborate decorations on the outside. One depicts a struggle between an old man and a younger man, in which the old man seemed to be the victor. Historians guess that it depicts the struggle that follows the death of a king. The other cup shows a barren landscape in which a griffon tears apart the bodies of a horse and a stag, and historians think it represents a Scythian story of the underworld.

In all the grave sites, there are many depictions of animals because of the apparent importance of animals in Scythian religion. Animals adorn knife hilts and pins. There are small animal figures of lions, tigers, and bears (oh my!), as well as hundreds of gold panther beads once sewn onto clothing.

The biggest question about Scythian gold is who made it? Modern historians are still trying to find the answer. Some of the gold objects seem influenced by Chinese art, while others appear to have Greek origins. It's possible that the answer depended on the particular tribe. While gold had value across tribes, some tribes may have obtained gold art objects through trade while others had their own artisans. No evidence has been found of Scythian gold-working other than the objects themselves. Some of the ornaments were produced solely for funerary rites, with rough edges that would have been impractical in daily life, while others show use before burial. While these objects provide insight into Scythian culture, they also guide us towards new questions about the people who buried them.

Gold plaque with panther, probably for a shield or breast-plate, 13 in/33 cm long, end 7th-century BC

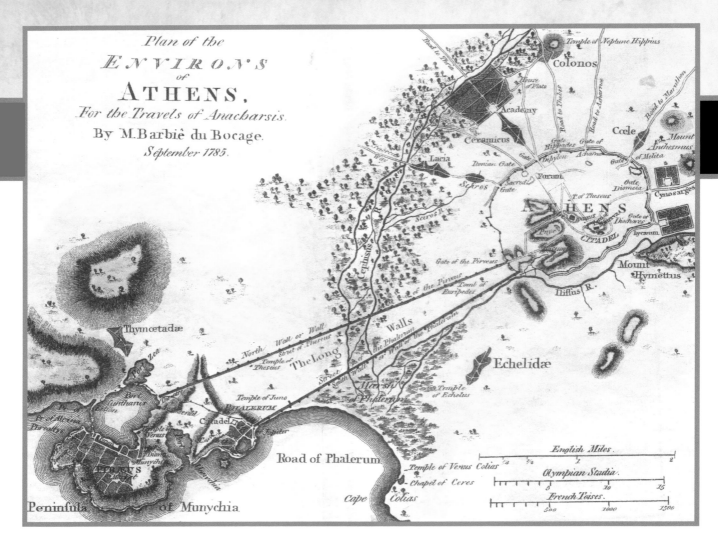

Athens became the birthplace of democracy in 508 BC/BCE and remained a democracy until the Macedonian king, Philip II, conquered the city 180 years later. Although no longer an independent city-state, Athens remained the Mediterranean center of wealth and culture for centuries. Even after Rome conquered Athens in the Battle of Corinth in the second century, Athens was granted special status as a "free city" because of the reputation of its schools. Academics and merchants alike relied on Greek language to communicate throughout the Mediterranean region. Dramatists, philosophers, mathematicians, poets, and historians made their home in Athens and greater Greece, many of whom remain well-known today. In fact, much of our knowledge of the ancient world comes from the writings of Greek historians such as Herodotus. Math students still know the name of Pythagoras and use his famous theorem.

The Roman respect for Greek culture led to a deep influence on Roman culture from religion to art to politics. The gods (mostly) had different names in Roman beliefs, but many of the myths and traditions were either similar or exactly the same. In fact, Julius Caesar cited an ancient myth to emphasize the closeness of Greco-Roman culture: the myth of Aeneas and the founding of Rome. Romans took more than religion from the Greeks, however. Greek art became popular in Rome and wealthy Roman families commissioned works of art from Greek sculptors and artists, while Latin poets and musicians took inspiration from Greek musical forms and modes.

Athenians originated the idea of a representative government with works like Plato's *Republic,* a source of inspiration for the Roman Republic and later the revolutionaries of the English, American, and French revolutions. Great thinkers such as John Lilburne, Thomas Jefferson, and Jean-Jacques Rousseau borrowed ideas from Greek political thinkers to support their own causes.

If you ever visit Washington, D.C, the capital of the United States, you will see Greek influences in every

ATHENS

direction. Of course, the representative government of the United States evolved from Greek democracy, but those same ideals inspired the architecture and art of the capital city. The Capitol Building itself resembles a Greek or Roman temple, as does the Supreme Court with its Corinthian, Doric, and Ionian columns and statues of senators and judges in Greco-Roman clothing. This style of architecture, called "neoclassical," shows up in other places in the city and nation, including the Lincoln and Jefferson memorials, the Baltimore Basilica, the University of Virginia, the Bank of Pennsylvania, the Richmond Capitol Building, the Fairmount Waterworks in Philadelphia, and Thomas Jefferson's home, Monticello.

Around the world during this time, the Olmec empire was fading away. The Persians attempted to expand their empire with varying degrees of success; they attacked Greece multiple times, and the Athenians and Spartans were kept busy either defending Greece in the Persian Wars or attacking each other in the Peloponnesian Wars. A Sanskrit scholar named Yaska wrote one of the earliest known grammar manuals. The Zhou dynasty ruled in China and the Jomon period in Japan came to an end.

The Acropolis imagined in an 1846 painting by Leo von Klenze

Mathematics

Some of the most interesting people in Greek history were actually mathematicians. Not only were they revolutionaries when it came to the role of proof and deductive reasoning in math and science, and not only did they invent the entire field of geometry, they were also fascinating people who lived in a world of drama and excitement.

One of the most well-known mathematicians was Pythagoras, who lived in the 6th century BC/BCE. He established a school that blended together math and mysticism. It was unusual for the time, but men and women were both welcome at the school and treated as equal scholars. Everything at the school was communal, and those who lived and worked there were expected to follow a set of rules. Pythagoras, who believed in

the transmigration of souls (that souls were reborn into the bodies of other people and animals), enforced vegetarianism for all of his followers. Some of his other rules sound a bit bizarre today. The Pythagoreans were forbidden from using iron to stir a fire, from touching a white rooster, or from marrying a woman who wore gold, just to name a few restrictions. They also followed the edict that "all is number" or "God is number," and practiced a form of number worship. Each number had a specific meaning and identity. One, the number of reason, was the generator of all other numbers. Two meant opinion, three meant harmony, and four meant justice. The sum of these number is ten, which they called tetractys and considered the most holy of numbers. Pythagoras is most famous for the Pythagorean Theorem: In a right triangle, the length of the hypotenuse squared is equal to the sums of the square of each of the other two sides. Pythagoras may or may not have discovered this theorem independently, but he certainly is responsible for its fame. His student, Hippasus, made another important discovery, that certain numbers cannot be expressed as a fraction, such as the square root of two. However, the Pythagorean cult was so strict that they drowned Hippasus when he tried to make his discovery public.

Another famous Greek school was the school established by Plato. Although Plato is most famous today as a philosopher, the motto over the entrance to Plato's academy demonstrates his role as a mathematician: "Let no one ignorant of geometry enter here." In fact, Plato saw mathematics as a branch of philosophy, and the first ten years of the fifteen year course of study at his academy included an in-depth study of mathematics. Plato identified the shapes that became known as the five Platonic solids: tetrahedron, octahedron, cube, icosahedron, and dodecahedron. In addition to his own contributions to mathematics, Plato's academy fostered the next generations of mathematicians.

The mathematician Euclid, also known as the Father of Geometry, likely studied at the academy for a time before continuing his studies in the Egyptian city of Alexandria. Euclid wrote the first and most influential math textbook of all time: *Elements*. It included all of the mathematical knowledge developed up until that time, such as mathematical formulas, Euclid's five general axioms and five geometrical postulates, the golden ratio, and the beginnings of number theory. It was the definitive text for over 2,000 years, and laid out the foundations of what we call Euclidean geometry.

FURTHER READING

All Ages
The Librarian Who Measured the Earth by Kathryn Lasky. Eratosthenes, the librarian in the title, was born in a Greek city in modern day Libya. He studied in Athens and ended up as the librarian of the famous library in Alexandria, Egypt. It's a great narrative to discuss the spread of Greek influence.

Ages 5-9
What's Your Angle Pythagoras? By Julie Ellis. While not truly biographical in any sense of the word, it's a great introduction to Pythagoras' famous theorem.

Of Numbers and Stars: The Story of Hypatia by D. Anne Love. Hypatia actually lived in Egypt, but in Hellenistic (Greek-influenced) Egypt and followed the traditions of Greek scholarship. She's notable as one of the first famous female scholars and lived in the late 4th and early 5th centuries AD/CE.

Ages 10-15
Where Is the Parthenon by Roberta Edwards. Readers will learn about the Golden Age of Athens, Pericles, and the city of Athens while they read about the construction of the Parthenon.

The Death of Socrates by Jean Paul Mongin. For those interested in philosophy after reading about Greek thought, this little volume is a good introduction to Socratic thought as it follows Socrates during his last days.

The Death of Socrates, by Jacques-Louis David (1787)

Philosophy

Greek philosophy provided the basis for early Islamic philosophy, Renaissance thought, and the Age of Enlightenment. Although it may have had its origins in the literature and thought of ancient Near East mystics, Greek philosophy marks a beginning of true reasoning thought in Greece and the surrounding areas.

The earliest philosophers, known today as the Pre-Socratics, began searching for explanations about the world that did not rely on traditional mythology. Some of these philosophers criticized or mocked mythological beliefs and explanations. They spent a great deal of time discussing the cosmos and its origins. While not all of them rejected belief in the Greek pantheon, they did move away from anthropomorphizing the gods (making them seem human) and giving them human faults. They also began developing the skill of rhetoric, or argument.

Out of these philosophers rose Socrates, who founded much of modern philosophy and gave his name

to the Socratic Method. In the Socratic Method, which he used extensively, argumentative dialogue is used to stimulate critical thinking and find flaws in an argument. He became unpopular as a result of his extensive use of this technique because it often made his opponents seem foolish or ignorant. Socrates largely focused his arguments on morality and virtue, yet the Athenian government accused him of leading youth astray and failing to pay proper homage to the gods. He was executed in 399 BC/BCE for these crimes. Socrates' execution is famous, not just because of his own fame, but because of the method. He was forced to drink a cup of brewed hemlock, a deadly poison.

Socrates had many followers during his lifetime, and Plato was one of the most famous. He made contributions in mathematics and philosophy, and like Socrates, saw the importance of dialogues in stimulating thought. We have no evidence that Socrates wrote down any of his arguments, but Plato wrote many dialogues arguing different points of view. In most of them, it is difficult to pinpoint what Plato himself thought because he did such a thorough job of covering

The Cave

Imagine prisoners who have spent their whole lives in a cave. In the cave, they cannot turn around, they can only stare at the smooth rock walls. Behind them, a fire is burning and a walkway passes by where each day people and animals travel carrying all sorts of objects. They create shadows on the wall that the prisoners look at. This is the only way that the prisoners have ever experienced the world.

Now imagine that one of the prisoners is freed, and he leaves the cave for the first time. He begins to experience the world in a new way: looking at plants, animals, and people. Seeing colors and textures and undistorted shapes. Smelling, touching, and tasting things for the first time. He realizes that the shadows he saw were not the whole world, just confusing images cast on the wall.

Now imagine he runs back to the cave to tell his friends what he has learned. But they cannot recognize him. He appears to them as only a distorted shadow, and his words do not make sense. The prisoners cannot understand the world outside the cave, but this does not make the world any less real.

Plato's "Allegory of the Cave", drawing by Markus Maurer

both sides of the argument. One of his most famous pieces of writing is the allegory of the Cave, which is all about point of view.

One of the students at Plato's academy was the philosopher Aristotle, who went on to tutor a young Alexander the Great. Like Plato, Aristotle wrote extensively. He wrote treatises on ethics, politics, logic, nature, theology, and physics. While the Greeks are famous for their contributions in mathematics, Aristotle was the most influential person in the study of physics until the work of Newton.

These men lived thousands of years ago, yet we still know their names and build on the work that they started, using some of their own techniques for learning. They were a truly influential group.

Plato told many allegories, stories that were meant to teach us something about the world or help us think about things in a new way. Read the allegory of The Cave and discuss what Plato might have been trying to teach his followers.

Baths

The ancient Greeks placed great value on hygiene and had elaborate bathing rituals for cleanliness, therapeutic purposes, and as a social activity. Some bathing practices would be familiar to us today, while others might sound a little strange. Today, many people enjoy using scented bath salts, fancy bath bombs, or bubble bath. The Greeks also used mineral salts, like Epsom salts, in their baths, along with scented herbs such as bay laurel, lavender, fir, pine, and juniper. Sometimes they used the fresh herbs and other times they used essential oils. Sometimes they even put clay in their baths, a practice which is having a resurgence today. It was considered especially beneficial to drink a cup of peppermint or elderflower tea before getting into the bath. That sounds like a good recipe for relaxation. On the other hand, the Greeks believed that cold water was the best for cleanliness and that hot water should be reserved for therapeutic baths. They also had a bathing ritual that had some ingredients not usually found in the modern bathroom. After wetting their bodies, they smeared themselves with a mixture of pumice and ash.

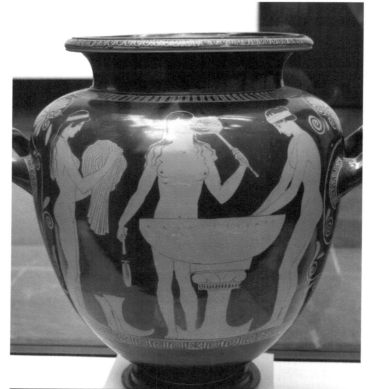

Three young women bathing. Side B from an Ancient Greek Attic red-figure stamnos. Photo by Bibi Saint-Pol.

It might sound counterproductive but the process makes a bit more sense if you know that ash is used in some methods of soap making. Then they covered themselves with olive oil. Finally, the scraped everything off with a curved metal scraper called a strigil. The strigil also scraped off the underlying dirt and grime. But don't worry, by the second century AD/CE, they were also using soap.

The Romans are famous for their elaborate public baths, but the Greeks also had public bathing spaces.

The earliest bathers simply used whatever body of fresh or salt water was nearby, but they also built bathing structures around these natural bodies of water. Certain springs, especially warm springs, were associated with deities and considered especially healing. Indoors, the bather might sit in a wooden or marble bathtub while a slave poured hot water over his or her neck and shoulders. Sponge baths using a small basin were also popular.

No matter what kind of bath they took, the Greeks bathed regularly. At least some sort of basic cleaning ritual took place daily before the noontime meal, which was the main meal of the day. Public bath houses were often located near gymnasiums so that athletes could wash off their sweat after physical exertion. The Spartans, known for their physical prowess, particularly enjoyed steam baths rather than full immersions.

Were the Greeks unusual in the ancient world for their enjoyment of cleanliness and hygiene? Well, not particularly. The earliest public baths originated in the ancient Indian city of Mohenjo-daro. The Chinese and Romans both placed importance on cleanliness. Even in ancient Britain, the people brushed their teeth at a minimum. On the other hand, when the Roman Empire collapsed towards the end of the ancient era, public baths fell into disrepair and gradually disappeared. The beginning of the Middle Ages signalled a decline in European hygiene, at least temporarily.

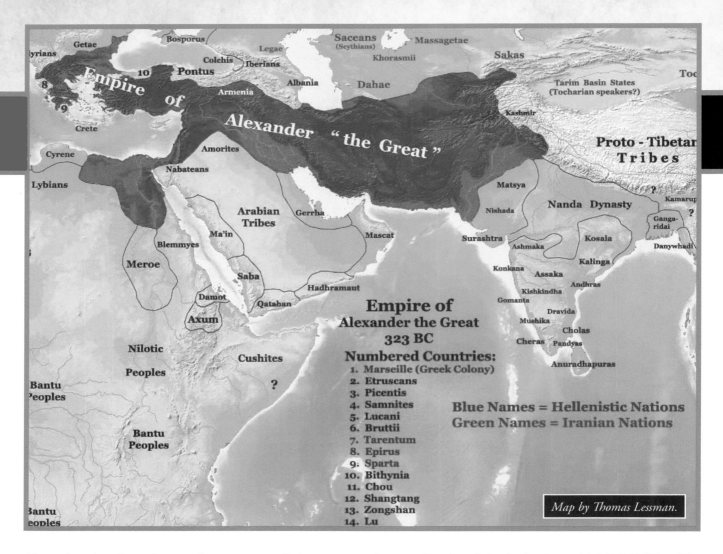

Map by Thomas Lessman.

Empire of Alexander the Great 323 BC

Numbered Countries:
1. Marseille (Greek Colony)
2. Etruscans
3. Picentis
4. Samnites
5. Lucani
6. Bruttii
7. Tarentum
8. Epirus
9. Sparta
10. Bithynia
11. Chou
12. Shangtang
13. Zongshan
14. Lu

Blue Names = Hellenistic Nations
Green Names = Iranian Nations

Alexander the Great has a place as one of the most famous conquerors in history, and with good reason. His empire, while short-lived, existed on three continents (Europe, Africa, and Asia). He crossed mountains, seas, and deserts with a fighting army of 37,000 men, along with scientists and other learned men, artisans, women, and children. In fact, as many as 10,000 babies were born during his eleven year campaign into Asia.

Even Alexander's origin story has elements of fantasy. His father, King Philip, was said to be descended from Heracles (Hercules), while Alexander's mother, Olympias, claimed to be a descendant of the great hero Achilles. Perhaps it is no wonder that Alexander slept with a copy of the Iliad (the epic poem by Homer which starred Achilles) under his pillow while on his Asian campaign. From childhood, Alexander was trained for greatness. He hunted lions, learned to play the lyre, took lessons from Aristotle, and practiced with the weapons he would use as an adult. Always ambitious, he acted quickly to secure his place on the Macedonian

throne after his father's death in 336 BC/BCE. He quickly extinguished a smoldering rebellion in the city of Thebes, and by 334 BC/BCE Alexander was prepared to take on the Greeks' most hated enemies: the Persians.

Alexander believed that he was destined for greatness, both because of his mythical ancestry and because of predictions from the Oracle at Delphi. Although his campaign into Asia began as a vendetta against the Persians, he had greater plans from the beginning. Always desiring eternal fame, he had historians, poets, sculptors, painters, and musicians accompany his army in order to both record and glorify his accomplishments. His pride may have been his downfall, as he began to act as if he truly were a god. While the Egyptians and Persians may have been happy to treat him as such, his behavior angered his Macedonian and Greek followers. Although he wished to continue further into India, the rest of his army and officers refused to follow him. Perhaps if he had not alienated his followers,

ALEXANDER THE GREAT

they would have continued following his orders without question. During the journey home, he died of a fever (possibly malaria).

In the end, Alexander's campaign did have long-lasting influence and he succeeded in achieving enduring fame. He founded around twenty cities, and brought Greek influence as far as Pakistan and India. His name appears in histories of Egypt, the Scythians, Mesopotamia, and India. Sometimes, it seems that not a single Old World culture escaped Alexander's influence.

Even where Alexander did not lead an army, you can still find the touch of his influence. He met with ambassadors from the African kingdoms of Cyrene and Ethiopia, from Carthage, and from Italy (perhaps even Rome). Iberian ambassadors came from Spain and Scythians from the Asian steppes. The Celts came from Gaul and Germany.

Alexander's life continued to have influence even after his death. Greek culture flourished throughout the Middle East for another 300 years. His withdrawal from India created a power vacuum eagerly filled by Chandragupta Maurya as he built the Mauryan Empire.

Statue of Alexander the Great in Thessaloniki, Makedonia, Greece. Photo by twins_2.

Alexander and the Great Gordian Knot

There are many legends around Alexander the Great's life and accomplishments. Some of these stories may have a basis in fact, but have grown into legends far beyond reality. Alexander himself spread the rumor that the Greek god Zeus was his true father.

Bucephalus

When Alexander was about twelve-years-old, a horse dealer named Philonacus came to Philip II's court. He was selling a magnificent horse for thirteen talents, an enormous sum. The horse, Bucephalus, was a huge, glossy-black stallion with a white star on his head and striking blue eyes. But Philip did not buy the animal—Bucephalus reared and bucked, and no one could tame him. Alexander asked for the chance to try, and his father agreed. The boy removed his fluttering cloak and approached the stallion and turned it towards the sun, so that the animal could no longer see its own shadow. Bucephalus had been afraid of his own shadow and the movements of the men's flowing cloaks. The horse was now Alexander's to command, and he rode Bucephalus into many battles until the horse was killed in the Battle of the Hydaspes, in modern-day Pakistan. The distraught Alexander founded a city in his horse's memory, calling it Bucephala.

The legends grew after Bucephalus' death. Some stories say that Alexander and his mount were born at the same moment and died at the same moment. Others say that the Oracle at Delphi predicted that the man who rode a horse with the mark of an ox's head on his haunch, a horse named Bucephalus, would become the king of the world.

The Gordian Knot

Long before Alexander, the kingdom of Phrygia found itself without a king. The people consulted an oracle. "The first man to ride up to the temple in an oxcart shall be your king." A poor farmer named Gordias soon appeared, and was crowned king according to the directions of the oracle. He founded the city of Gordium and tied the oxcart to the temple with an intricate knot that became known as the Gordian Knot. An oracle predicted that the man who could unravel the knot would become the king of Asia (for the ancients, this meant Asia Minor or Anatolia). After Gordias' death, his son Midas assumed the throne. You may have heard of him: he wished for the power to turn everything he touched into gold. But that's a story for another time.

Nearly a thousand years passed, and the knot remained solidly tied. Alexander arrived in Gordium on his march of conquest, and decided that he must be the one to unravel the knot. Try as he might, he could not find an end to unravel. He took his sword and sliced the knot in half, unraveling it permanently. Alexander went on to conquer large portions of Asia, including Anatolia. Was it all because of his victory over the Gordian knot?

Alexander the Great Cutting the Gordian Knot, Giovanni Paolo Panini (1692–1765).

100

Advances In Ancient Medicine

The century before Alexander the Great's birth was an exciting time for medical science. Hippocrates, a Greek physician known as the father of modern medicine, made huge strides in changing medical care from a superstitious and mystical practice to a science based on reasoning and observation. Alexander's army benefited from the treatment of doctors using new medical techniques.

Hippocrates is credited with originating the "Hippocratic Oath" that doctors still take today: a set of promises to practice medicine in an ethical way. The Caduceus symbol, which is still used as a symbol of healing and medicine, also originated from ancient Greece and was used at this time.

Still, Hippocrates also made some mistakes. Without any knowledge of bacteria, viruses, or other micro organisms, he came up with a different explanation of sickness: The Four Humors. In this theory, there are four basic substances in the body: blood, yellow bile, black bile, and phlegm. In a healthy person, they are in balance. If the humors become imbalanced, the person becomes ill. Treatment revolves around trying to bring the humors back into balance. An imbalance can also cause psychological problems such as aggression or melancholy. According to the Greeks, the Romans, and later Muslim and Western European medical communities, each humor has a corresponding season, element, organ, quality, and temperament.

These ancient doctors believed that the liver produced blood, which was associated with the element air and the season of spring. Blood was described as warm and moist. The resulting temperament is sanguine, or hopeful and carefree.

Yellow bile came from the spleen, and was warm and dry as befitted a humor associated with fire and summer. An imbalance of yellow bile resulted in a choleric temperament, or someone who is quick to anger or aggressive.

The Greek word for black bile (melaina khole) gave us our word melancholy, the associated temperament for the humor produced by the gallbladder.

Cold and dry, black bile is linked to autumn and the earth.

Phlegm, produced by the brain and lungs, is a cold and moist winter humor associated with water and phlegmatic, or thoughtful, temperament.

This flawed theory led to treatments that sometimes worked, and sometimes did not. A fever, as a hot dry disease, would be diagnosed as an excess of yellow bile. To reduce yellow bile, the physician would prescribe a cold bath to increase phlegm, the opposite of yellow bile. Other methods included changes in diet, activity, or exercise. For a cold, caused by excess phlegm, the doctor would prescribe wine. If the blood humor was to blame, blood letting purged the excess humor.

The theory of the four humors was used in medical practice for 2,000 years. It wasn't until the 19th century that it was disproved and fell out of favor.

Hippocrates, engraving by Peter Paul Rubens, 1638.

Ancient World Gestures

Do you ever shake a friend's hand or blow your mom a kiss? You have the peoples of the ancient world, including Alexander the Great, to thank!

The tradition of shaking hands in greeting dates back to Ancient Greece. The Greeks shook hands with those they considered equals, in a demonstration that weapons were not necessary.

A myth has been going around for years that in the great battles of the gladiators, in ancient Rome, spectators would put out a thumbs up if they wished the Emperor to spare the life of a gladiator, and a thumbs down if they wanted to see him killed. In truth, any show of a thumb indicated that the spectator wished to see the gladiator killed.

Kissing (on the lips) has its origins in ancient India and spread to the rest of the world through... you guessed it... Alexander the Great. Alexander's generals brought the practice back with them after his conquest of India. The practice of blowing kisses originated in Mesopotamia as a way to beg favor of the gods and became a mark of honor toward a higher-ranking individual.

Relief inscribed stele with the Samain honorary decree. The relief depicts Hera and Athena, patron-deities of Samos and Athens respectively, clasping hands. Photo by Marsyas.

FURTHER READING

All Ages
Alexander the Great by Demi. Demi writes beautifully illustrated biographies for children. These biographies often include mythical tales about the subject's life. The narratives are easy to read and the gilded illustrations are absolutely gorgeous.

Ages 5-9
You Wouldn't Want to Be in Alexander the Great's Army: Miles You'd Rather Not March by Jacqueline Morley. I love this humorous series that tells it like it was about life in the past. In this case, Morley describes life in Alexander's army from the beginning of the campaign until its bitter end. The cartoonish illustrations are engaging while you can't help but gasp at some of the events that happened along the way.

Ages 10-15
Who Was Alexander the Great? By Kathryn Waterfield and Robin Waterfield. Part of the Who Was? Series of biographies, this book hits all the major points of Alexander's life in an entertaining and engaging way.

Alexander the Great by Philip Freeman. This biography is not written for children, and thus should be previewed or reserved for mature students as it discusses topics not suitable for all young readers. However, I include it for its level of detail and supreme readability.

Alexander Mosaic (c. first century AD), ancient Roman floor mosaic from the House of the Faun in Pompeii showing Alexander fighting king Darius III of Persia in the Battle of Issus.

War Elephants

Have you ever read or seen the *Lord of the Rings*? Then you might be familiar with Tolkien's oliphaunts, gigantic animals with tusks used in battle. Tolkien was a scholar of medieval literature, where he probably read about "olifants." Medieval European scholars described them as big enough to carry a castle on their backs, enemies of dragons, and extremely long-lived with lifespans as long as 300 years! You are probably more familiar with the modern spelling: elephant. While you know most of those "facts" were not true, they were used in battle, especially in India.

We don't know exactly when the people of ancient India started training elephants for war, but they were important as far back as the Indus Valley civilization. They appear on many seals found at Harappa and Mohenjo-daro. By the time Alexander the Great invaded India, war elephants were a standard part of the army. King Porus hoped to intimidate Alexander with these massive beasts, but relied too heavily on the unpredictable animals. Alexander went for the other units of the army, and then the elephants panicked and lost control. Alexander won the day, for the time being. As he moved east, he left men called satraps behind to control newly conquered lands. After Alexander's death, Chandragupta Maurya (Ashoka's father) took advantage of the new situation and offered 500 war elephants to one of the satraps, in exchange for control over four provinces. The satrap gladly accepted. Chandragupta had plenty to spare: he had around 9,000 elephants!

Throughout Indian history, the elephants were used by royalty and military leaders to give a commanding view of the battlefield. During the Mauryan dynasty, they were also used by archers. Three archers rode, with two shooting from the front and one from the rear. During other periods, the elephants carried up to seven riders including archers, swordsmen, and banner carriers. They were outfitted with armor and trained to attack with tusks, trunk, feet, head, and even tail. The animals were so important that anyone who killed an elephant would be put to death.

So how did they perform in battle? They were definitely intimidating and did a lot of damage when on the rampage. On the other hand, they were moody and unpredictable. Often, they caused damage to their own side or ran away from battle, causing other troops to retreat. One tactic involved giving them alcohol, which made them even more aggressive, but probably made them even harder to control. While sitting high on an elephant gave a great view, it also turned the rider into a great target. Despite their shortcomings, they remained important military vehicles, even into the Middle Ages. They did not fade away completely even then, because they were such status symbols. During the American Civil War, the King of Siam (Thailand) offered to send elephants to aid the Union.

In the circle: Hannibal's celebrated feat in crossing the Alps with war elephants passed into European legend: detail of a fresco by Jacopo Ripanda, c. 1510, Capitoline Museums, Rome. Photo by José Luiz Bernardes Ribeiro.

Background: A 17th-century depiction of the mythological war of Lanka in the ancient Indian epic Ramayana, showing war elephants. Source British Library.

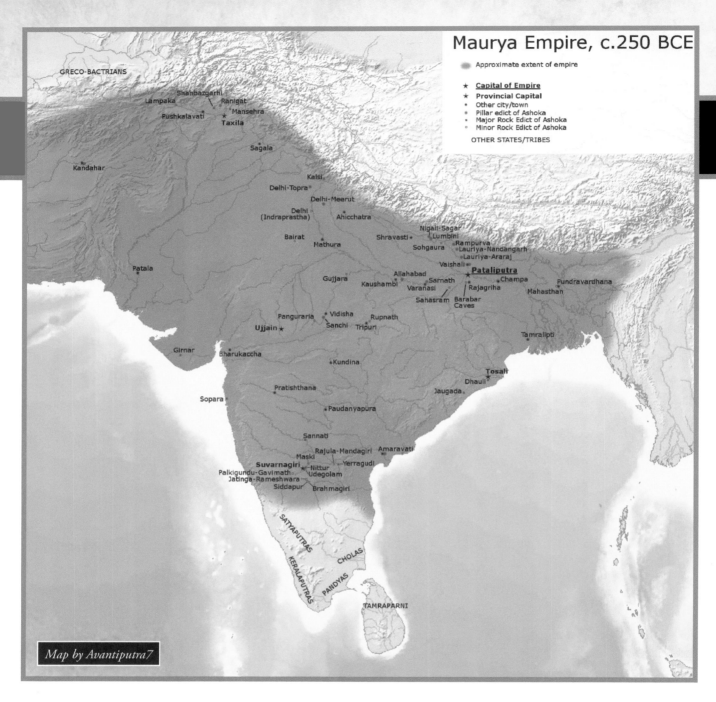

Maurya Empire, c.250 BCE

- Approximate extent of empire

- ★ **Capital of Empire**
- ★ **Provincial Capital**
- • Other city/town
- • Pillar edict of Ashoka
- • Major Rock Edict of Ashoka
- ◦ Minor Rock Edict of Ashoka

OTHER STATES/TRIBES

GRECO-BACTRIANS

Shahbazgarhi
Lampaka
Ranigat
Mansehra
Pushkalavati
Taxila

Kandahar

Sagala

Kalsi
Delhi-Topra
Delhi-Meerut
Delhi (Indraprastha)
Ahicchatra

Nigali-Sagar
Lumbini
Bairat
Shravasti
Rampurva
Mathura
Sohgaura
Lauriya-Nandangarh
Lauriya-Araraj
Vaishali

Patala

Gujjara
Allahabad
Sarnath
Pataliputra
Champa
Pundravardhana
Kaushambi
Varanasi
Rajagriha
Mahasthan
Sahasram
Barabar Caves

Panguraria
Vidisha
Rupnath
Ujjain
Sanchi
Tripuri

Tamralipti

Girnar
Bharukaccha
Kundina

Tosali
Dhauli

Pratishthana
Jaugada

Sopara

Paudanyapura

Sannati

Rajula-Mandagiri
Amaravati
Maski
Suvarnagiri
Nittur
Yerragudi
Palkigundu-Gavimath
Udegolam
Jatinga-Rameshwara
Siddapur
Brahmagiri

SATYAPUTRAS
KERALAPUTRAS
CHOLAS
PANDYAS

TAMRAPARNI

Map by Avantiputra7

Ashoka was the third king of the Mauryan Empire in India, one of the largest empires in the world at the time. Ashoka's grandfather, Chandragupta Maurya, founded the empire in the wake of the departure of Alexander the Great's armies. The empire quickly grew to encompass most of the Indian sub-continent, and perhaps as far as parts of Nepal and China. However, all expansion ceased during his grandson Ashoka's reign. After the Battle of Kalinga, Ashoka felt deeply moved by the enormous loss of life. He converted from Hinduism to Buddhism and dedicated the remainder of his reign to peace, preservation of life, and spreading Buddhist teachings (which were about two hundred years old by this time). He ordered the erection of enormous stone pillars throughout the empire, inscribed with his edicts against unnecessary killing and behaviors he considered sinful. Many of these were topped by sculptures, especially lions, which were important symbols of the empire. Although he promoted Buddhism, he did not discriminate against those who continued practicing Hinduism and had a policy of religious tolerance.

There followed a series of weaker kings after Ashoka's reign, and the Mauryan kingdom fell into decline. Likewise, Buddhism fell out of favor as Hinduism

MAURYAN EMPIRE

regained dominance. Finally, the empire became part of the Indo-Greek kingdom. By the time the Mauryan empire ended in 185 BC/BCE, many elements of modern Indian culture were already present. The caste system, a strict designation of social class, began during the Vedic period leading up to the Mauryan Empire and continues to an extent in India today. The sari and dhoti, both garments still worn in India today, appeared during this period as well. Today, Hinduism is the world's third largest religion after Christianity and Islam, and it is the dominant religion in India and Nepal. Seven to eight percent of the world's people are Buddhists, most of whom live in Asia.

At the same time as this first great Indian Empire, China's first dynasty came into power: the Qin Dynasty that gave its name to the country. Rome and Carthage were embroiled in the Punic Wars, and Greek kingdoms dominated their section of the Mediterranean region. Around the time that the Mauryan Empire ended, the Hopewell Culture appeared in North America and the kingdom of Teotihuacan in Mexico was founded.

FURTHER READING

All Ages
Ramayana: Divine Loophole by Sanjay Patel. The *Ramayana* is sacred to Hindus today. This gorgeously illustrated retelling is by a Pixar illustrator who grew up with the *Ramayana* as part of his cultural identity and wanted to share it with a wider audience.

Buddha by Demi. Demi's signature gilded illustrations accompany the history and legends of the Buddha's life.

Ages 5-9
Ancient India: Maurya Empire by John Bankston. In addition to a detailed history of the Indus River civilization and the Maurya Empire, this book also includes directions for a terracotta craft and a historical recipe for rice pudding. It is out of print, but available on the Epic app. Check your library and favorite used book seller.

Ages 10-15
Chandragupta Maurya: The Determined Prince by Adurthi Subba Rao. One of many graphic novels in a series about the history and folklore of India, this one in particular covers Chandragupta Maurya's rise to power. Another volume is called *Ashoka*. They are available in paperback and Kindle versions.

The Ancient World: Ancient India by Allison Lassieur. Beautiful illustrations, photographs of artifacts, and detailed maps all bring the history of India to life in this volume. It covers the earliest civilizations in Harappa and Mohenjo-Daro, all the way up through the Mauryan Empire.

Ashoka's Famous Monologue

When Ashoka's father, Bindusara, died in 273 BC/BCE, Ashoka went to battle against his own brothers to ascend to his throne. According to the text Ashokavadana, he "managed to become king after getting rid of the legitimate heir by tricking him into entering a pit filled with live coals."

He spent the first eight years of his reign known as "Ashoka the Fierce," a king with a wicked nature and bad temper. Finally, his attention turned towards the independent kingdom of Kalinga. The war against Kalinga claimed over 200,000 lives and left Kalinga in a state of devastation. This war that claimed so many lives would also change Ashoka's life forever.

After seeing the aftermath of a battle first hand he wrote:

"What have I done? If this is a victory, what's a defeat then? Is this a victory or a defeat? Is this justice or injustice? Is it gallantry or a rout?... Do I (kill the innocent) to widen the empire and for prosperity or to destroy the other's kingdom and splendor? Are these marks of victory or defeat? Are these vultures, crows, eagles the messengers of death or evil?"

People say that he was filled with dwandwam, or doubt. Overwhelmed with remorse, Ashoka resolved to change his life and his kingdom. He converted to Buddhism, studying peace and even becoming a vegetarian. He traveled throughout his kingdom, spreading his messages of peace and encouraging conversion to Buddhism.

Ashoka and his two queens, in a relief at Sanchi. The identification with Ashoka is confirmed by the similar relief from Kanaganahalli inscribed "Raya Asoka". Photo by Photo Dharma.

Ashoka pillar at Vaishali. Photo by Bpilgrim.

Hinduism vs Buddhism

The three largest religions in India today are Hinduism, Islam, and Christianity. At the time of Ashoka, however, nearly all Indian people were Hindu. Islam and Christianity did not exist. Buddhism was a couple of hundred years old when Ashoka converted from Hinduism to Buddhism. What do Hindus and Buddhists believe? What's the same? What's different?

Hinduism	Buddhism
Founded in 2000 BC/BCE or before	Founded around the 5th century BC/BCE
No single founder, based on older beliefs including those from the Indus River Valley civilization	Founded by Siddartha Gautama, who was born in either 563 or 480 BC/BCE* and based on his Four Noble Truths about the nature of suffering. He was raised as a Hindu.
Belief in many gods and goddesses; sometimes a belief that they are all images of a single god	No emphasis on belief in a deity. Some continue to believe in deities, others do not believe in any gods.
Belief in reincarnation	Belief in reincarnation
Provides guidelines for life to work towards freedom from the cycle of reincarnation	Provides guidelines for life to work towards freedom from the cycle of reincarnation
Promotes ahimsa, or nonviolence	Promotes ahimsa, or nonviolence
Four goals in life: duty, prosperity, pleasure, and freedom from rebirth	Eightfold path: accept teachings of Buddha, give up worldly things, speak with kindness and truth, avoid violence, living minimally and without harm, guarding thought, mindfulness, and meditation
Many religious texts, including the Vedas which are the most important	The main religious texts are the Sutras, or teachings of the Buddha. Some traditions use other texts.
Often vegetarian	Often vegetarian
Primary religion in India, home to most of the world's Hindus	Most of the world's Buddhists live in China.
Many different sects with different beliefs and practices	Many different sects with different beliefs and practices
A living tradition that continues to evolve	A living tradition that continues to evolve

*Sources are inconclusive about his birth year.

Stories of Hinduism and Buddhism

The Hindu Creation Story

Here's the tricky part: There isn't just one! Different religious texts have different stories of creation. Because Hinduism is a collection of beliefs and not all sects share the same beliefs, different creation stories even contradict each other. Some say that the source of creation was a golden egg. Others say that the god Vishnu was floating in an ocean of milk on a serpent's stomach when a lotus bloomed from his navel and revealed the god Brahma, who went on to create everything else. Hinduism also has a cyclical view: the world/universe has been created and destroyed many times. Today, as well as long ago, different Hindus have different beliefs about the world's origins. Most Hindus today believe in evolution. They see it as compatible with their beliefs in reincarnation. They compare the evolution of fish to the god Vishnu's first incarnation, which was as a fish. There are also Hindu creationists who reject evolution and believe that humans appeared fully formed trillions of years ago. My favorite Hindu description of creation is from the Rig Veda:

"Who really knows, and who can swear, How creation came, when or where! Even gods came after creation's day, Who really knows, who can truly say When and how did creation start? Did He do it? Or did He not? Only He, up there, knows, maybe; Or perhaps, not even He."

Life of The Buddha

While scholars generally agree that Siddhartha Gautama was a real person, most of the facts are lost in history. Here is one story of his life:

Once there was a prince named Siddhartha Gautama. His parents believed that he would be a great ruler someday. They felt that they should protect him from all suffering, and he grew to adulthood without ever seeing pain, illness, or death. Then one day, some time after his marriage to a princess, he left the palace and saw an old man. He had never seen the effects of aging before and begged his charioteer, Channa, to explain what he had seen. Once Channa had explained, Siddhartha took further trips from the palace to see the suffering of life. He saw a sick man, a rotting corpse, and an ascetic. An ascetic was a holy man who lived very simply, without material possessions, and fasted often. Siddhartha himself was so depressed by these sights that he became an ascetic himself, sneaking away from his comfortable life in the palace. He meditated under teachers but felt that asceticism was not the answer either. He sat under a tree and meditated for 49 days until he reached "Enlightenment," or rather, found the answers to solve life's suffering. At age 35, he became "Buddha," which meant awakened one. Several members of his family became his disciples. The Buddha spent the rest of his life traveling and teaching.

The Victory of Buddha

111

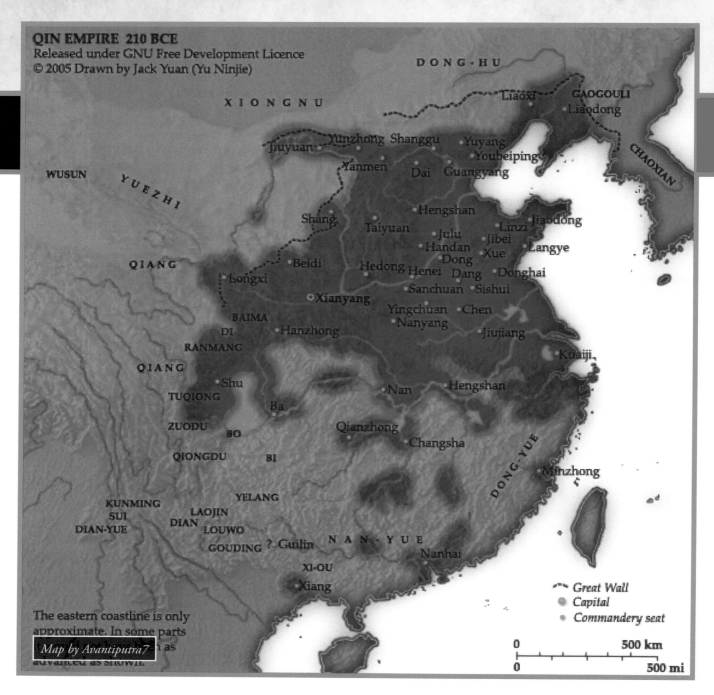

DONG-HU

XIONGNU

Liaoxi · GAOGOULI
Liaodong

Jiuyuan · Yunzhong Shanggu · Yuyang

CHAOXIAN

WUSUN

YUEZHI

Yanmen · Dai Guangyang
Youbeiping

Shang · Hengshan · Jiaodong
Taiyuan · Linzi
Julu · Jibei
QIANG · Handan · Xue · Langye
Beidi · Dong
Longxi · Hedong · Henei · Dang · Donghai
Sanchuan · Sishui
Xianyang
BAIMA · Yingchuan · Chen
DI · Nanyang
Hanzhong · Jiujiang
RANMANG
QIANG · Kuaiji
Shu · Nan · Hengshan
TUQIONG
Ba
ZUODU · Qianzhong
BO · Changsha
QIONGDU · BI
DONG-YUE
YELANG · Minzhong
KUNMING
SUI · LAOJIN
DIAN-YUE · DIAN · LOUWO · NAN-YUE
GOUDING ? Guilin · Nanhai
XI-OU
Xiang

Great Wall
Capital
Commandery seat

0   500 km
0   500 mi

The eastern coastline is only
approximate. In some parts
Map by Avantiputra7 as
advanced as shown.

Emperor Qin Shi Huangdi united all of China in 221 BC/ BCE. Before this time, China had been divided into several warring states. China's first dynasty, the Shang dynasty, ruled over most of Northern China during the Bronze Age. The Shang kings believed that they were given power to rule by heaven. During the Shang dynasty, the Chinese people invented a writing system. Most of the people were peasants, who grew food for everyone else. Common foods included soy beans, ginger (which disguised the taste of old meat), noodles, rice, mung beans.

Artisans used bronze, silk, jade, and clay to make goods for the people, including weapons and clothing. Silk, made from the cocoons of silkworms, was a carefully guarded secret in China for thousands of years.

After the Shang Dynasty came the Zhou dynasty, which brought a period of warfare. Iron replaced bronze as the main material for weapons and tools. The philosopher Confucius was born during this period and wrote down his thoughts about how to make the kingdom more peaceful. He elevated kindness, respect, and obedience

EMPIRE OF CHINA

as the highest virtues. His writings continue to influence China, even today.

Finally, in 221 BC/BCE, the king Zheng, who ruled over the Qin state, conquered all six major kingdoms and united them into one empire. He renamed himself Qin Shi Huangdi: Qin, for his kingdom; Shi, meaning the first; and Huangdi, meaning emperor and divine ruler. Qin, pronounced Chin, gave China its name. China remained a united kingdom, even after the emperor's death and the fall of the Qin Dynasty. The First Emperor was a harsh ruler, who used forced labor to begin building the Great Wall and who taxed heavily. Many of his subjects suffered from starvation as a result. He also did not tolerate disagreement, and burned books and executed scholars who spoke out against him. However, the First Emperor also established standardized currency and a system of weights and measures. He also chose the dragon as his emblem because it embodied wisdom, strength, and goodness. The association between emperors and dragons continued throughout China's history. In the end, Qin's harsh rule resulted in a peasant uprising and the beginning of the Han dynasty three years after Qin's death.

The Han dynasty marked the beginning of China's imperial civil service, which ran the country in service of the emperor for 2,000 years. After passing challenging exams, civil servants became the most honored citizens in China. Over the next thousand or so years, Chinese subjects designed some of the greatest inventions the world had ever seen. The Chinese discovered how to create iron, make a basic compass, and make a wheelbarrow. Chinese ships had rudders for steering not much later, and long before European ships had such devices. Paper appeared shortly after the fall of the Qin dynasty. Although used medicinally in the Qin dynasty, tea would not become a popular beverage until around 750 AD/CE. Printed books became widely available by 1050 AD/CE, around 400 years before the invention of the printing press in Europe. The Chinese people invented playing cards, pick up sticks, dice games,

Chinese checkers, and a version of football. They had an advanced medical system, which relied heavily on acupuncture and herbal medicine. Today, western doctors are learning about integrating these traditional medicinal practices with modern medicine.

During the 3rd century BC/BCE, when Qin Shi Huangdi ruled over China, great changes took place in other parts of the world. In India, Ashoka tired of warfare and converted to Buddhism. Migrants from Korea brought bronze, tool-making, and new agricultural techniques to Japan. Rome warred with Carthage throughout the century. The Epi-Olmec civilization in Mexico developed writing and a calendar.

Science in Ancient China

Have you ever enjoyed fireworks? Owned a piece of gold-plated jewelry? Maybe you've gone geocaching with a compass or watched a hot air balloon? You probably didn't know that you had the Ancient Chinese to thank. Beginning more than 2,500 years ago, scientists in Ancient China started making truly wonderful discoveries and inventions. They constructed crossbows, sun compasses, magnetic compasses, and even the world's first seismograph (for detecting earthquakes.) They mixed mercury with gold and silver to make plating possible, and they invented gunpowder, used in fireworks and explosives. Many of these inventions spread by means of the Silk Road, an important trade route that linked China, Europe, and Africa from the 2nd century BC/BCE to the 3rd century AD/CE.

Confucius

Ah, Confucius. Perhaps no name better conjures up the image of a wise man spouting short and wise phrases such as "do unto others as you would have others do unto you." However, if you traveled back to 6th century China, where the famed wise man grew up, he would not respond to that name. As a child, his family called him Kong Qiu. When he grew up, his courtesy, or adult name, became Zhongni. He was known by many names over China's long history. Kong Fuzi, or "Grand Master Kong" became Latinized to Confucius in the sixteenth century by Jesuit missionaries. The Chinese also called him the Master; the Laudably Declarable Lord Ni; the Extremely Sage Departed Teacher; Great Sage; First Teacher; and Model Teacher for Ten Thousand Ages. All these titles convey Confucius' great influence and importance in Chinese history.

He was born in the Lu province to a military officer father who died when Confucius was only three years old. He grew up in poverty under the care of his mother and was educated in the six arts in schools for the common people. The six arts were Rites, Music, Archery, Charioteering, Calligraphy, and Mathematics. A man who mastered all six would be considered a perfect gentleman. Although he was poor and went to common schools, Confucius belonged to the shi class, somewhere between the aristocracy and the common people. He married at age 19 and started his government career in his 20s. He quickly became influential in provincial politics, as neighboring dukes vied for power. His own career waxed and waned with the tides of power, but he remained respected for his intelligence and judgement. He finally returned home to Lu in his sixties and became a teacher to a group of 70 or so students. His teachings later became the foundations of Confucianism, a school of thought that guided the Chinese people for centuries.

Confucius believed in the importance of personal and governmental morality. Morality and loyalty came before all other values. He even placed an importance on good judgment over simply following rules. He believed that the family provided an example of ideal government, with respect of children for their elders and the respect of wives for their husbands. He hoped China would someday be united and ruled by one virtuous monarch. Today, scholars debate about whether Confucianism is a form of "secular morality" or a religion. Most of his teachings provide guidance for the present, but did occasionally write about the afterlife and Heaven. One Confucian teaching shows up in many world religions: "Do unto others as you would have others do unto you."

Confucius, gouache on paper, c. 1770

Photo by zetter

The Great Wall of China

The Great Wall of China went through some big changes over time. The original wall, constructed at the time of Emperor Qin, was made in a completely different way than the great wall we all know today. Workers used wooden troughs to hold dirt which they packed down with rods that had one flattened end. Workers continued this until the dirt became as hard as concrete! The result was a strong but not very beautiful wall. Later the original Qin wall was first reinforced and then bricked over during the Ming Dynasty to make the great wall that has become such a historic icon.

To respond to a popular myth: No, you cannot see the Great Wall of China from space.

FURTHER READING

All Ages
The Emperor's Silent Army: Terracotta Warriors of Ancient China by Jane O'Connor. I love this book for the illustrations alone, but it also gives great biographical information about Qin Shi Huangdi.

Ages 5-9
Ming's Adventure with Confucius in Qufu by Li Jian. This is a bilingual English and Chinese book about a little boy who travels back in time to learn directly from Confucius. Ming makes connections between the teachings of Confucius and today in an adorably funny way.

Ages 10-15
DK Eyewitness Books: Ancient China by Arthur Cotterell. Anytime DK Eyewitness has a book on a subject, I know it's going to be worth checking out. The photographs of real artifacts draw kids in, and it's easy to either digest a few facts at a time or dive into all the captions in great detail.

"Et tu, Brute?"
"Beware the Ides of March."
"Friends, Romans, Countrymen."
"It was Greek to me."

Likely, you've heard at least some of those lines before, from William Shakespeare's play *Julius Caesar.* But did the Bard write history or did he write fiction? The truth is a bit complicated. Shakespeare based his play on Plutarch's *Lives of the Noble Grecians and Romans,* written around two hundred years after Caesar's assassination,

but the Bard used a great deal of artistic license. For one, the play mentions a mechanical clock, which is a complete anachronism. Second, although the assassination did take place on the Ides of March (March 15), we do not have any record of Caesar receiving a warning from a soothsayer. Certainly the monologues are entirely spun from Shakespeare's imagination. On the other hand, it is possible that Caesar's last words were "You too, my son?" At the very least, the legend of Caesar's final words predated Shakespeare's version. Many of the events in the play are true to history, but

JULIUS CAESAR

condensed from a period of several years to a period of only a few weeks.

We know a great deal about Julius Caesar, partially because he wrote a great deal about his own military career. Gaius Julius Caesar was born July 12, 102 BC/BCE to patrician parents who traced their ancestry back to the goddess Venus. Despite his noble birth into Rome's most elite class, his family did not possess much in the way of wealth. Like most patrician boys, he received an education in reading, writing, history, philosophy, arithmetic, and rhetoric. Rhetoric, or the art of public speaking, was considered vital for a boy who would likely pursue a career in politics. When Caesar was only fifteen years old, his father died. In order to support himself, he took a minor diplomatic post and then joined the army. From the beginning, he showed great ambition and confidence. While sailing on a ship to the Greek city of Rhodes to study rhetoric under Apollonius Molon, pirates attacked the ship and took Caesar prisoner, hoping to hold him for ransom for the great sum of twenty talents, more than a year's wages for the average Roman. Caesar laughed bravely and told the pirates that he was worth at least fifty talents. He then proceeded to threaten the pirates, telling them that one day, he would execute them all. When Roman officials paid the ransom, Caesar was released and immediately made good on his threat. Despite a lack of official authority, Caesar seized several ships and

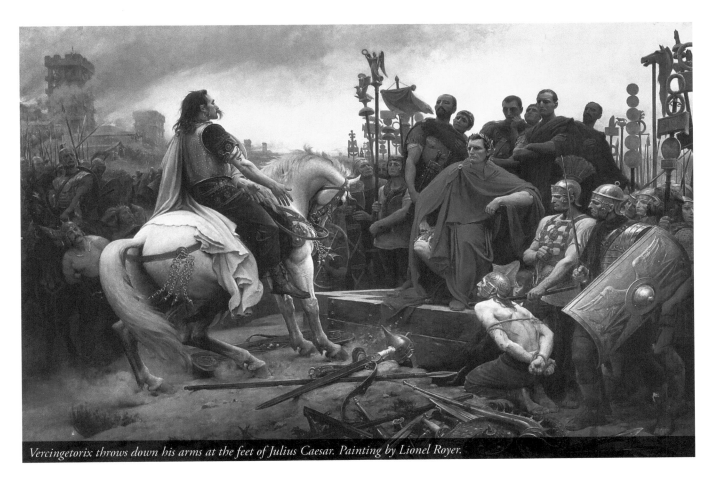

Vercingetorix throws down his arms at the feet of Julius Caesar. Painting by Lionel Royer.

chased down the pirates. He executed them all, which made him quite popular in Rome. Caesar spent years working his way up through Roman society, combining a knack for popularity with carefully calculated political moves. He made friends with the wealthiest senator in Rome, and used the money to organize spectacles for the citizens of Rome such as chariot races and gladiatorial fights. This senator, Crassus, also provided the opportunity to become one of Rome's two consuls in 59 BC/BCE. As consul, he was one of the two most powerful men in Rome. After his one-year term ended, his rise to power continued with military conquests in Gaul (France) and raids in Britain. However, back in Rome, political intrigue worked against Caesar and he returned to Italy only to go to war. Eventually, he traveled onto Egypt where he became romantically involved with the famous queen Cleopatra.

At last, Caesar victoriously returned to Rome, where he was declared the Dictator of Rome. Although he was not the first to be appointed to this position, he was the first to be made Dictator for life. He now had vast powers, enough to reshape the government by removing power from the patricians and improving conditions for the plebeians (Roman commoners). His decisions made him popular with the ordinary citizens, but less popular with those who had lost power as a result. The final straw came in 44 BC/BCE. Caesar made his dictatorship hereditary, ordering that the position would be passed onto his nephew, Octavian, after Caesar's death. At the same time, he wished the Senate to grant him a royal title. In March of that year, Caesar called a meeting of the Senate. Upon his arrival in the Senate building, one group of Senators fell upon him, stabbing him dozens of times.

Caesar's death plunged Rome back into warfare between the conspirators, who wished the government to return to the Republic it had been before Caesar's dictatorship, and Caesar's nephew (Octavian) and friend (Mark Antony). Neither side was without its own conflict, and both sides dissolved into their own civil wars. The Roman Republic had been destroyed, and the Roman Empire rose from its ashes. Caesar's role in the demise of the Roman Republic and the establishment of the Roman Empire cannot be overstated. The Roman Empire eventually became one of the largest empires in history, stretching from western Europe to North Africa to the Middle East. At its peak, Rome ruled between one-sixth and one-fourth of the world's population and encompassed five million square kilometers. Rome's language, Latin, is the ancestor of the

Things Named After Julius Caesar

July
The month of July was named for Julius Caesar, and the month of August named for his nephew and successor, Caesar Augustus. It's why September, October, November, and December mean seventh, eighth, ninth, and tenth months but are actually the ninth through twelfth months.

Julian calendar
The Julian calendar introduced the 365 day year, with 366 days every fourth year. The Gregorian calendar (used today) is based on the Julian calendar but with additional leap year rules to compensate for the actual length of a tropical day.

Cesarean birth (disputed)
Some sources say that Caesar was born by cesarian birth. Others argue that it was an ancestor. Others say that it's not related to his birth at all and merely a coincidental name.

Caesarea (various cities in various countries)
Just as Alexander the Great founded several cities named Alexandria, so Caesar left his mark on the lands he conquered.

Other rulers (Caesar, Kaiser, and Czar)
Caesar Augustus was not the only ruler to take the name Caesar. His own stepson took the name, and it soon became a title rather than a family name. In Germanic languages the title became Kaiser and in Slavic languages, such as Russian, it became variations of Czar. Even Arabic took Caesar's name and used it as a word for palace: Qas'r.

Things Not Named After Julius Caesar

Caesar Salad
Caesar Salad was actually named for an Italian restaurateur working in San Diego who invented the salad in the 1940s. His name was Caesar Cardini.

Romantic languages (French, Spanish, Portuguese) and remains in use within the Catholic Church to this day. Although the Roman Republic may have already been in decline, Caesar's dictatorship put the final nails in the coffin and paved the way for this empire to rise.

During his lifetime, Julius Caesar set foot on three continents during his military conquests. He traveled to Gaul, Egypt, and Asia Minor. Likewise, his influence spread throughout those lands. What else was going on in the world during the 1st century BC/BCE (also called the last century BC/BCE)? The entire Mediterranean region came under Roman control, and Egypt became part of the empire as well. In the East, the China's Han dynasty fell and the royal court was plunged into chaos. At the very end of the century, a new millennium began. At least, it was a new millennium by our count, using the supposed date of the birth of Jesus of Nazareth. For the Romans, it was just the year 753 AUC.

Julius Caesar. Commissioned in 1696 for the Gardens of Versailles. Photo by Marie-Lan Nguyen.

When In Rome...

If you traveled back in time to ancient Rome, you might find some really tasty things to eat... and you might be offered food that would make you reconsider your hunger. By our modern tastes, it would be safest to eat the foods enjoyed by an average Roman citizen or even the poorest inhabitants of the city. They ate fruits and vegetables familiar to us today: apples, pears, grapes, peas, beans, lentils, onions, garlic, lettuce, and cucumbers. They also ate bread made of wheat or barley, and occasionally cheese or eggs. Meat was expensive, and the poor wouldn't have eaten much meat at all. Those who were better off might occasionally have fish or chicken. While most Romans ate food prepared at home, those with a little money could eat out at taverns or at fast food stands called hot spots. These weren't too different than food stands today, with a menu board offering chicken, sausage, ham, or bread. Romans often started the day with hot water, piped into the city through aqueducts. Although the water was generally clean to start with, and boiled, it did come through pipes lined with lead which caused mental and physical health problems. If you needed a bit of a boost, you could drink a honey refresher, a drink made of honey, water, and pepper. Adults of all classes drank wine, but most ordinary people drank a cheap wine called pasca. Pasca tasted like vinegar, even when it was diluted with water.

If you were very fortunate (or unfortunate?) you could be invited to a Roman banquet. Offerings might include ostrich brains, peacock tongues, stuffed dormouse, or lamprey eel. Often, wealthy Romans used their banquets to show off their wealth through creative cuisine. You may have heard of a turducken (a chicken stuffed inside a duck stuffed inside a turkey). The Romans had a cowpigooseducken. They stuffed a chicken inside a duck inside a goose inside a pig inside a cow, and then cooked the entire cavalcade of meats together. Money did have benefits, as wealthy Romans had the money to send charioteers up into mountains for snow slushies and chilled asparagus.

No matter where you are a guest, you are expected to bring your own napkin. And don't be surprised by the dining arrangements. Romans ate reclining on sofas, and used their fingers to eat rather than knives and forks.

Caesar Says

"Alea iacta est."
The die has been thrown.

"Divide et impera."
Divide and conquer.

"Ignavi coram morte quidem animam trahunt, audaces autam illam non saltem advertunt."
The cowards agonize about death, the brave don't even notice it.

"Veni. Vidi. Vici."
I came. I saw. I conquered.

"Fere libenter homines id quod volunt credunt."
Men willingly believe what they wish.

The Tusculum portrait, perhaps the only surviving sculpture of Caesar made during his lifetime. Photo by Gautier Poupeau.

The Laurel Wreath

The laurel wreath has held symbolism since the time of the Greeks, who associated laurel with the god Apollo. The Romans adopted the laurel wreath along with other elements of Greek culture and tradition. In Rome, the laurel wreath symbolized peace, eternity, victory, unrequited love, and a supreme ruler. The wreath represented a divine blessing from the Gods and was often seen in images of the goddess Victoria. It may seem strange that one symbol could stand for both peace and victory, but for the Romans, peace was achieved through victory over their enemies. The Corona Triumphalis, a wreath or crown of laurels, was the highest medal in Roman society. The Senate bestowed this wreath upon victors upon their return from war. Julius Caesar received this particular honor, and it became linked to the emperors who ruled after his death. Emperors from Octavian Augustus to Justinian minted coins of their likeness wearing laurels.

FURTHER READING

All Ages
Cleopatra by Diane Stanley. Learn about Caesar and Mark Antony through the lens of their famous lover. The book handles the subject delicately, but preview the ending for sensitive learners who may find her death disturbing.

Ages 5-9
Hero Journals: Julius Caesar by Nick Hunter. Written in Caesar's first person voice, Hunter describes Caesar's upbringing, rise to power, and tragic fall.

Ages 10-15
Who Was Julius Caesar? By Nico Medina. A biography in the illustrated "Who Was" series, the text provides details about Caesar's life and the culture from which he came, saw, and conquered.

The following link will take you to a list of Caesar's works and their English translations:
http://www.forumromanum.org/literature/caesarx.html

The Death of Caesar, Jean-Léon Gérôme, 1867

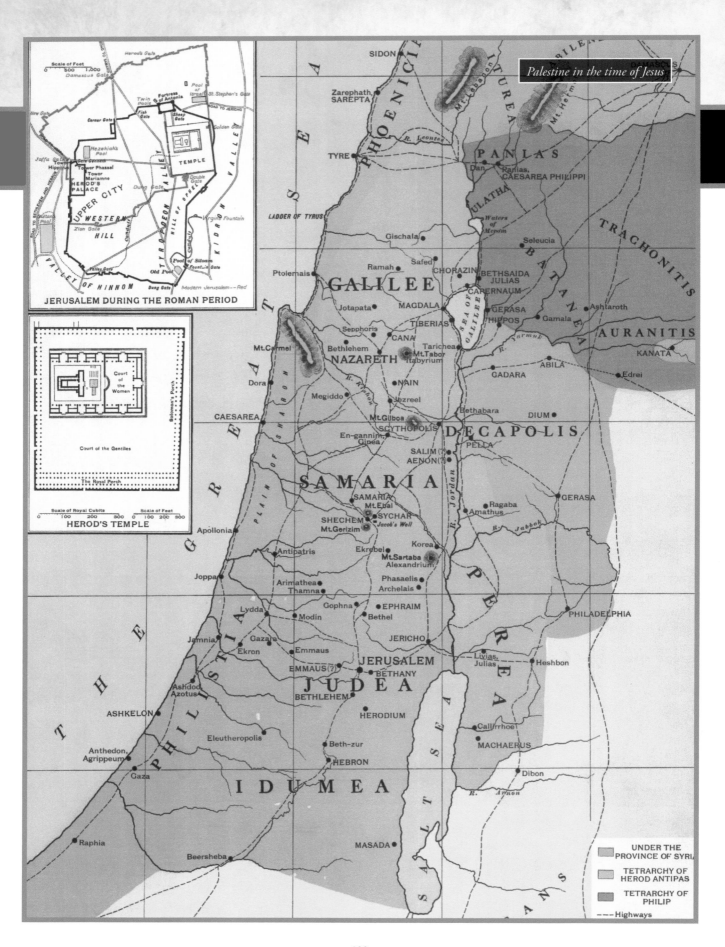

Palestine in the time of Jesus

JERUSALEM DURING THE ROMAN PERIOD

Jerusalem inset labels:
Scale of Feet
0 500 1,000
Herod's Gate
Damascus Gate
Pool of Israel
St. Stephen's Gate
Twin Pools
Fortress of Antonia
ROAD TO JERICHO
New Gate
Corner Gate
Fish Gate
Sheep Gate
Golden Gate
Hezekiah's Pool
Jaffa Gate
Gate Gennath
Hippicus
TEMPLE
Tower Phasael
Tower Marianne
Double Gate
KIDRON VALLEY
HEROD'S PALACE
Dung Gate
TYROPOEON VALLEY
HILL OF OPHEL
UPPER CITY
WESTERN HILL
Virgin Fountain
Zion Gate
Conduit
Sultan's Pool
Pool of Siloam
Valley Gate
Old Pool
Fount'in Gate
Dung Gate
VALLEY OF HINNOM
Modern Jerusalem—Red

HEROD'S TEMPLE

Temple inset labels:
Court of the Women
Court of the Gentiles
Solomon's Porch
The Royal Porch
Scale of Royal Cubits
0 100 200 300
Scale of Feet
0 100 200 300

Main map labels:
SIDON
DAMASCUS
PHOENICIA
Zarephath, SAREPTA
ITUREA
Mt. Hermon
TYRE
R. Leontes
PANIAS
Dan, Panias, CAESAREA PHILIPPI
LADDER OF TYRUS
ULATHA
Waters of Merom
TRACHONITIS
Gischala
Seleucia
Ptolemais
Ramah
Safed
CHORAZIN
BETHSAIDA JULIAS
BATANEA
GALILEE
CAPERNAUM
Ashtaroth
Jotapata
MAGDALA
SEA OF GALILEE
GERASA
HIPPOS
Gamala
AURANITIS
Sepphoris
CANA
TIBERIAS
KANATA
Mt. Carmel
Bethlehem
Taricheae
Mt. Tabor Itabyrium
NAZARETH
ABILA
Edrei
Dora
NAIN
R. Kishon
GADARA
Megiddo
Jezreel
R. Jordan
Mt. Gilboa
Bethabara
DIUM
CAESAREA
SCYTHOPOLIS
DECAPOLIS
En-gannim, Ginea
PELLA
PLAIN OF SHARON
SALIM (?)
AENON (?)
SAMARIA
Ragaba
SAMARIA
Mt. Ebal
Amathus
GERASA
SYCHAR
SHECHEM
Jacob's Well
Mt. Gerizim
R. Jabbok
Apollonia
Korea
Ekrebel
Mt. Sartaba Alexandrium
Antipatris
PEREA
Joppa
Phasaelis
Archelais
Arimathea
Thamna
THE GREAT SEA
Gophna
EPHRAIM
PHILADELPHIA
Lydda
Bethel
Modin
Jamnia
Gazara
JERICHO
Livias, Julias
Heshbon
Ekron
Emmaus
JERUSALEM
EMMAUS (?)
BETHANY
Ashdod Azotus
JUDEA
BETHLEHEM
ASHKELON
HERODIUM
Eleutheropolis
Callirrhoe
Beth-zur
MACHAERUS
Anthedon, Agrippeum
HEBRON
Dibon
Gaza
SALT SEA
IDUMEA
R. Arnon
Raphia
MASADA
Beersheba
PHILISTIA

Legend:
UNDER THE PROVINCE OF SYRIA
TETRARCHY OF HEROD ANTIPAS
TETRARCHY OF PHILIP
--- Highways

122

CHRISTIANITY

Imagine that you are a resident of a village in the region between the Jordan River, the Dead Sea, and the Mediterranean River: Palestine. It's the 749th year after the founding of the city of Rome, and you live in the Roman Empire. Your parents and grandparents grew up during a violent and unstable time. Now, things are more peaceful. You have a Jewish king named Herod. It has only been a decade or so since Julius Caesar became emperor and was assassinated, and now Augustus Caesar reigns as emperor. Herod answers to Caesar.

You and most of your neighbors are Jewish. It is a strange time for your people. Some of the priests have started their own sects because people are having a hard time agreeing about how to be both Jewish and a Roman citizen.

A baby is born in your village. This baby will change the world. The baby's name is Jesus.[1]

For two thousand years, Christians have believed that Jesus was the son of God. Here is a short story about Jesus's life according to Christian beliefs.

Two thousand years ago, an angel appeared to a woman named Mary and told her that she was going to have a baby. Mary was surprised because she was not yet married. She was engaged to a man named Joseph. The angel told Mary that the child would be the son of God. An angel appeared to Joseph, telling him to take Mary as his wife even though the child she carried was not his own. Mary and Joseph traveled to the town of Bethlehem, where she gave birth to the baby Jesus.

Mary and Joseph were Jewish, and Jesus studied religion with teachers called rabbis. When he grew up, he traveled with a group of followers, called disciples, teaching people about God and performing miracles such as healing the sick. Some of his speeches made people angry because he criticized the way they did things. The Romans arrested him for causing rebellions and executed him by crucifixion, which is hanging someone on a cross. He died on the cross and was buried. On the third day after he died, his friends went to his tomb and found that it was empty. Soon afterwards Jesus appeared to them and told them that he had risen. He had sacrificed his life to pay the price for all the evil things people had ever done, and ever would do, so that people who loved God could be happy with him in heaven after they died.*

We don't have much physical evidence about the details of Jesus's life. Most of the information we have comes from the New Testament of the Bible, the sacred text of Christians. There are four sections, or books, that tell about the life of Jesus and are called the Gospels. The Gospels are Mark, Matthew, Luke, and John. All the books were written by followers who lived after Jesus. At first stories about Jesus's life and death were shared orally and we don't know exactly when or by whom they were written down. Mark was written sometime between 65 and 70 AD/CE. It's possible that the author of Mark was able to talk to people who knew Jesus but we don't know for sure. The other Gospels were written a little bit later, between 85 and 90 AD/CE for Matthew, and between 90 and 100 AD/CE for Luke and John. The writers all include some of the same stories, but each included different events and details. Mark, Matthew, and Luke are the most alike, but still have important differences. Only Matthew specifically tells the story of an unmarried woman becoming pregnant (although the angel visits in Luke, too). Mark and John don't mention Bethlehem, which has a strong connection with the Israelite King David and fits with the prediction of a Hebrew prophet called Micah that a shepherd from Bethlehem would become the new king of the Jews. John states that he knew Jesus personally, but he would have been writing when he was a very old man. Luke writes that his intention is to

---

1.   The name "Christ" came later. It comes from the Greek word, Christos, which means messiah. The Jewish people believe God will anoint a new king, called the Messiah.

compile the events that have been told to him by eyewitnesses.

The four Gospels included in the Christian Bible aren't the only Gospels, but they are the only ones accepted by Christian religious traditions. The only other documents written close to the time of Jesus were letters written around 65 AD/CE. They described the Last Supper (the meal that Jesus shared with his disciples before he was arrested) and his execution, but did not give details about his life. Everything written by Jesus's Jewish followers and early Christians reflects their own opinions and beliefs. It can be hard to sort out the truth without other evidence. The Romans did not leave behind records about Jesus from his lifetime, but by around 115 AD/CE, they were writing about Christians. One historian, Suetonius, wrote that Jews were banished from Rome around 50 AD/CE because a man he called "the Chrestus" was instigating disturbances in the Jewish community.

Sermon on the Mount, by Carl Bloch, 1877, depicts Jesus' important discourse

This lines up with events described in the Bible. Betwen 71 and 94 AD/CE, a Jewish-Roman historian named Flavius Josephus wrote a book called *Antiquities of the Jews*. Jesus of Nazareth is mentioned twice in this history of the Jews, but one of the instances may have been added in a later translation. No original copies of the document have survived and the oldest copies date back to the 6th century AD/CE.

Was Jesus a historical figure? Most scholars agree he was. Less than 50 years passed between the time when Jesus probably died (between 26 and 36 AD/CE) and when Roman historians started writing about the Christian community. That's not much time for an entire religious movement to pop into existence without a charismatic leader. Still, there have been movements since the 18th century to prove that Jesus did not exist and was made up by writers like Paul (another author of the Bible). Other scholars consider Jesus to be similar to historical figures such as Confucius, Hammurabi, Pythagoras, Socrates, and Siddhartha Gautama. We know they existed, but so many legends

have built up around them that it is difficult to sort out fact from fiction.

While Jesus himself was Jewish and most of his early followers considered themselves Jewish, eventually his teachings formed the basis of a new religion. This new religion, Christianity changed the world. There are over two billion Christians in the world today. Jesus is also considered a prophet by the nearly two billion Muslims in the world. The Jewish people still wait for their messiah to come, but many see Jesus as an important teacher. Even our historical dating system dates back to the birth of Jesus, even when we change our terminology. BC means Before Christ, and AD means *Anno Domini*, or Year of Our Lord. While the terms BCE (Before Common Era) and CE (Common Era) are more inclusive terms, they are still lined up with the Christian calendar tradition.

Christian Beliefs

Christians believe that Jesus is the son of God and that Jesus died so that people who love God while they are alive can be happy with him in heaven after they die. Today, there are many kinds of Christians that can be divided into three large groups: Orthodox, Protestant, and Catholic. While they all interpret the Bible differently, they share a single creed. A creed is a statement of faith. The Christian statement of faith is called the Nicene Creed and it dates back to the fourth century.

The Nicene Creed
I believe in one God,
the Father almighty,
maker of heaven and earth,
of all things visible and invisible.
I believe in one Lord Jesus Christ,
the Only Begotten Son of God,
born of the Father before all ages.
God from God, Light from Light,
true God from true God,

begotten, not made, consubstantial with the Father;
through him all things were made.
For us men and for our salvation
he came down from heaven,
and by the Holy Spirit was incarnate of the Virgin Mary,
and became man.
For our sake he was crucified under Pontius Pilate,
he suffered death and was buried,
and rose again on the third day
in accordance with the Scriptures.
He ascended into heaven
and is seated at the right hand of the Father.
He will come again in glory
to judge the living and the dead
and his kingdom will have no end.
I believe in the Holy Spirit, the Lord, the giver of life,
who proceeds from the Father and the Son,.
who with the Father and the Son is adored and glorified,
who has spoken through the prophets.
I believe in one, holy, catholic and apostolic Church.
I confess one Baptism for the forgiveness of sins
and I look forward to the resurrection of the dead
and the life of the world to come. Amen.

Oldest extant manuscript of the Nicene Creed, dated to the 6th Century

Moses and Aaron with the Ten Commandments
(painting circa 1675 by Aron de Chavez)

Like Jewish people, Christians believe they should follow the Ten Commandments found in the Hebrew Bible. Here are the Ten Commandments as they appear in the New Revised Standard Version of the Bible

1. You shall have no other gods before me.
2. You shall not make for yourself an idol, whether in the form of anything that is in heaven above, or that is on the earth beneath, or that is in the water under the earth. You shall not bow down to them or worship them; for I the Lord your God am a jealous God, punishing children for the iniquity of parents, to the third and the fourth generation of those who reject me, but showing steadfast love to the thousandth generation of those who love me and keep my commandments.
3. You shall not make wrongful use of the name of the Lord your God, for the Lord will not acquit anyone who misuses his name.
4. Remember the sabbath day, and keep it holy. Six days you shall labor and do all your work. But the seventh day is a sabbath to the Lord your God; you shall not do any work—you, your son or your daughter, your male or female slave, your livestock, or the alien resident in your towns. For in six days the Lord made heaven and earth, the sea, and all that is in them, but rested the seventh day; therefore the Lord blessed the sabbath day and consecrated it.
5. Honor your father and your mother, so that your days may be long in the land that the Lord your God is giving you.
6. You shall not murder.
7. You shall not commit adultery.
8. You shall not steal.
9. You shall not bear false witness against your neighbor.
10. You shall not covet your neighbor's house; you shall not covet your neighbor's wife, or male or female slave, or ox, or donkey, or anything that belongs to your neighbor.

Finally, Christians follow the teachings of Jesus. In the New Testament of the Bible, there are many parables, or moral stories. Have you ever heard of the Golden Rule? According to the Golden Rule, you should treat others as you would like to be treated. In the Bible, Jesus tells a story about loving your neighbor as yourself. That sounds a lot like the Golden Rule. Many religious traditions have teachings similar to the Golden Rule. Other parables praise forgiveness, generosity and obedience to God.

126

Life of Early Christians

What was it like to be a Christian during the first three hundred years? In the beginning, it was not that different than being Jewish. There were many different Jewish sects that shared practices with Jesus' followers. In fact, for the first few decades, Jesus' followers still considered themselves Jewish. They worshipped on Saturday, the Jewish Sabbath. Like some other Jewish communities, they practiced baptism (purification through water). They worshiped only one god. They followed the teachings of the Hebrew Bible and circumcised their sons. They probably followed the same food restrictions as their fellow Jews. These Jewish Christians believed that the end of the world was near.

As the decades passed, Jesus' teachings became more popular. Gentiles, or non-Jews, began converting. These new Christians came from all parts of society; rich, poor, middle class, slaveholders, slaves, and free. When they joined the movement, Christianity became a separate religion from Judaism. The new religion grew quickly. It happened so quickly that scholars are still trying to figure out why. There are a lot of theories. The idea of eternal life in heaven might have sounded better than Roman ideas about the afterlife. Stories of miracles and healing may have convinced some people that Jesus and God were more powerful than Roman gods. Members of the lower classes may have been attracted to a faith that valued the most humble members of society. Christianity's stories of resurrection even fit with traditional Greek beliefs that immortality of the soul was linked with immortality of the body. When a head of household converted, his wife, children, and slaves all became Christian as well. Within about 70 years, there were about 40 Christian churches and Romans saw Christianity as a separate religion. Around this time, Romans started writing about Christians and Christianity. It also meant that Christians were no longer treated as Jews by the Roman government.

Roman law required all citizens to worship the Roman pantheon of gods. For Jews, it was against their religion to worship any god but their own. The Jews worked out a compromise with the Roman government

Chapel of Saint Ananias, Damascus, Syria, an early example of a Christian house of worship; built in the 1st century AD.
Photo by Titoni Thomas

so that they could pay a special tax instead of worshipping Roman gods. Eventually, the Romans decided Christians were a separate religion and not covered by this agreement. Christians did not have to pay the tax, but they could get in trouble if they did not worship all of the gods. Even so, the Empire did not have specific laws against Christians.

For long periods of time, the Empire extended religious toleration towards Christians. Sometimes local governors went after Christians if their other citizens got upset that they weren't obeying Roman law. Sometimes, people blamed Christians for their misfortune because they thought the gods were angry at not being worshipped. In 64 AD/CE, the Emperor Nero blamed Christians for a huge fire in Rome (even though he may have started it himself!). He had many Christians rounded up and executed. In 250 AD/CE, Emperor Decius decided to make all of his subjects prove their loyalty by making a sacrifice to the Roman gods. They had to make this sacrifice in front of witnesses and get a certificate as proof. The order did not target Christians specifically, but many Christians were imprisoned and executed for refusing to make the sacrifice. Jews were still exempt but Decius did not view Christianity as a religion. Emperor Diocletian was the last Emperor to persecute Christians across his Empire. He wanted to forbid Christians from being in the government or military. His advisor, Galerius, wanted to get rid of Christians. They went to the Oracle at Delphi for advice, and the Oracle told them that Apollo would not help them because there were too many impious people in the Empire. Diocletian began destroying churches and executing Church leaders. His actions backfired. Instead of frightening people, the executions inspired sympathy towards Christians. The martyred leaders inspired other Christians to stay strong in their faith. In 311, the very same Galerius became emperor and completely reversed his opinions. He issued the Edict of Serdica. It reversed all of Diocletian's anti-Christian laws. Why? The anti-Christian policies had clearly failed to discourage Christians. He decided a policy of peaceful tolerance was better for the Roman Empire. Then, in 313, Emperor Constantine issued the Edict of Milan which fully legalized Christianity. Roman persecution of Christians was over forever.

For the first 300 years, Christians did not have a unified statement of their beliefs and over the years different leaders promoted different ideas, forming sects within Christianity. Early Christians had fierce debates over whether these ideas were true. Some of them became part of the Christian faith and others did not. The ones that did not become part of the Christian faith were called heresies and Christians were forbidden to believe or teach them. Heresies from this time include Gnosticism, Montanism, Marcionism, Adoptionism, Docetism, Sabellianism, and Arianism. In 325 AD/CE Christian leaders held the Council of Nicea to clarify what Christians believed by writing those beliefs into a single statement called a creed. The Nicene Creed, which came from this council, remains the official statement of Christian belief, even today.

The Christ Pantocrator of Saint Catherine's Monastery at Mount Sinai, 6th century AD

FURTHER READING

A note to educators: Finding quality secular materials for children about Christianity can be a challenge. Please make sure you preview materials to make sure they are suitable for your family.

Ages 5-9
Meet Jesus: The Life and Lessons of a Beloved Teacher by Lynn Tuttle Gunney. This little picture book focuses on Jesus as a person. Readers learn the traditional story of Jesus' life without any supernatural elements. It does mention God within the context of Jesus' teachings but does not discuss the virgin birth or describe the resurrection as a factual event. Bible verses are cited at the bottom of the page.

The World Jesus Knew: A Curious Kid's Guide to Life in the First Century by Marc Olsen. NOTE: This book is not secular. However, it's included on this list because it is a fantastic living book with great diagrams, illustrations, and easily digestible text covering every aspect of life. The majority of the book does not focus on Christian theology. Educators, please preview the introduction and pg. 54-57 to evaluate according to your beliefs.

All Ages:
DK Eyewitness: Christianity by Philip Wilkinson. Another fantastic book from the Eyewitness series, this book uses the phrase "Christians believe" to clarify the differences between religious belief and historical fact. The photographs and sidebars are as engaging as always. The book covers Christianity up to the present day.

DK Eyewitness: Bible Lands by Jonathan N. Tubb. If you are looking for a broader context, this book is a great one to add to your reading list. It provides a great view into everyday life as well as the history of the Jewish people.

The World of the Bible: Biblical Stories and the Archaeology Behind Them by Jill Rubalcaba. This book is from National Geographic Kids. Each section has a straight retelling of a section from the Bible and insets of historical facts about the time period that are relevant to the story. Then there are additional sections that talk about the field of biblical archaeology from a fact-based perspective.

Collections of Bible Stories:
Bible literacy is an important skill, but there are few secular options. The book **Christian Mythology** by Chrystine Trooien is fully secular but is only available used. *The Complete Brick Bible for Kids: Six Classic Bible Stories* by Brendan Powell Smith is an option for younger learners who love LEGO, while teens might enjoy T*he Brick Bible: The New Testament: A New Spin on the Story of Jesus* also by Brendan Powell Smith. Please preview the latter as it is as graphic as one can get with LEGO. The Brick Bible options are directly adapted from the Bible without commentary.

National Geographic Treasury of Bible Stories is by Donna Jo Napoli, who has also written books about Greek, Egyptian, and Norse mythology. Her writing is beautiful and Christina Balit's illustrations are gorgeous. Sidebars give historical tidbits and notes about different translations. However, this book only includes Old Testament stories.

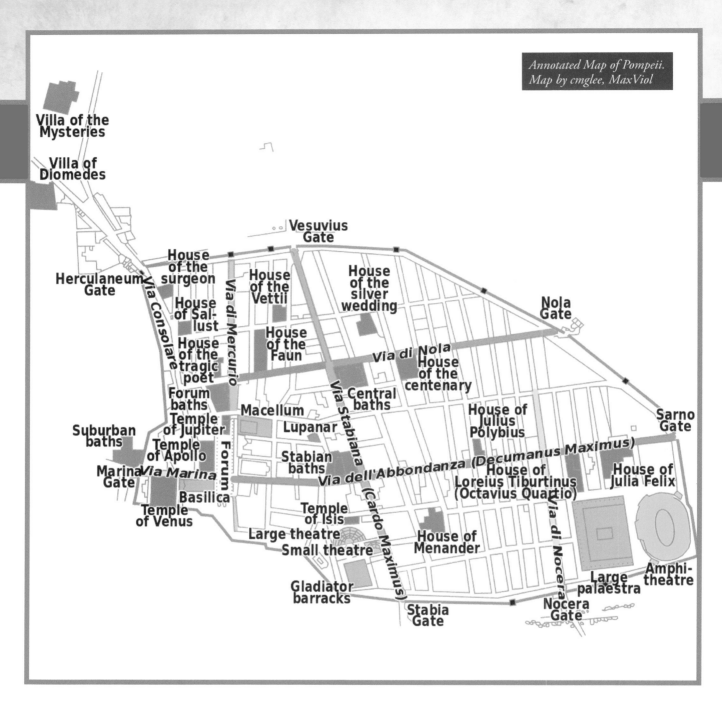

Villa of the Mysteries

Villa of Diomedes

Vesuvius Gate

Herculaneum Gate

House of the surgeon

House of the Vettii

House of the silver wedding

Nola Gate

House of Sallust

Via Consolare

Via di Mercurio

House of the tragic poet

House of the Faun

Via di Nola

House of the centenary

Sarno Gate

Forum baths

Temple of Jupiter

Macellum

Lupanar

Via Stabiana

Central baths

House of Julius Polybius

Suburban baths

Temple of Apollo

Forum

Stabian baths

Via dell'Abbondanza (Decumanus Maximus)

House of Loreius Tiburtinus (Octavius Quartio)

House of Julia Felix

Marina Gate

Via Marina

Basilica

Temple of Venus

Temple of Isis

Large theatre

Small theatre

House of Menander

Via di Nocera

Large palaestra

Amphitheatre

Gladiator barracks

Stabia Gate

Via Stabiana (Cardo Maximus)

Nocera Gate

Perhaps no natural disaster has been more captivating to people throughout history than the 79 AD/CE eruption of Mount Vesuvius, which buried the cities of Pompeii and Herculaneum. Archaeological excavations of the area date back to the 16th century, and Pliny the Younger's eyewitness account persists to this day. The volcanic eruption, which tragically destroyed two cities and took thousands of lives, also preserved evidence of daily life to an extraordinary degree. Hot ash, rock, and pumice buried people, streets, and buildings as they existed, and it happened so quickly that meals were left on tables and rooms were left untouched. Unique conditions even preserved the shapes of the people who were unable to escape. These discoveries provide a glimpse into life in Pompeii as it was on that fateful August day.

Pompeii was a center of trade for the Mediterranean, with many small shops and markets. It was particularly well-known for making cloth goods using wool from sheep raised just outside of the city. Others in the city wove linen. Wine makers, metal smiths, and bakers lived and worked in Pompeii. The city also served as a vacation spot during the warmer months, with luxurious public baths, restaurants, and large homes for the wealthy. Roman citizens walked in the streets, rubbing shoulders

POMPEII

with slaves brought from far-off lands who did everything from cleaning to doctoring. Pompeii, with a population of 20,000, was one of the largest cities in the Roman Empire. The gladiators were indeed the biggest celebrities in town.

The residents of Pompeii knew that Vesuvius was a volcano. However, despite the earthquakes that had become more frequent, they believed that it was dormant since the last eruption had occurred eight hundred years before. A severe earthquake had damaged the city in 62 AD/CE, but many stayed to rebuild the city. However, the eruption in August of 79 AD/CE destroyed the city that had stood for a thousand years and it disappeared, lost beneath piles of ash and rock, until an accidental discovery in 1594 led to plundering of the ancient city. Finally, in 1763, the site was identified as the lost city of Pompeii and formal excavation began in 1771.

Pompeii's destruction took place during the Pax Romana, a time of relative peace during the Roman Empire and often considered the prime heyday of the Empire, which controlled areas across Europe to Britain, North Africa, and the near East. It lasted from about 27 BC/BCE to 180 AD/CE. The Roman Republic had ended over a hundred years before, with the rule of Julius Caesar. According the Bible, Jesus Christ died approximately forty years before. It would take several hundred more years before Christianity would become the official religion of the Roman Empire. China was ruled by the Han dynasty for most of the first century, and Buddhism reached the Chinese people during this period. Christianity reached India in 52 AD/CE, and 64 AD/CE saw the first Roman persecution of Christians. The Mayan civilization experienced a mysterious collapse, many cities falling abandoned. Teotihuacan, an ancient city in Mexico, grew rapidly during this time, with the Pyramid of the Sun reaching completion between 100 and 150 AD/CE. The Zapotec civilization in Mesoamerica also expanded greatly throughout the century.

The Last Day of Pompeii. Painting by Karl Brullov, 1830–1833

Preservation of Pompeii

The preservation of Pompeii provides an incredible snapshot picture of life in the Roman Empire during the 1st century AD/CE. But how did this happen and what's happening today?

The eruption of Mount Vesuvius did not happen completely suddenly and without warning. The inhabitants of the cities at the base of the volcano had received warning in the form of an earthquake years before. In fact, many inhabitants left the area because of extensive damage from the earthquake, and much of the damage was not repaired before Vesuvius' eruption. Even when the great eruption began, inhabitants had warning and some had time to escape. The rumbling earth seemed to presage another severe earthquake, with tremors for four days leading up to a larger earthquake on the morning that the eruption began. Many ignored the smaller tremors, for they were somewhat used to seismic activity by this time. Then, around nine or ten in the morning, Vesuvius emitted a smaller explosion of ash, followed by a huge explosion at one in the afternoon. By 1:30 pm, the cloud of ash was 10 miles high and blown towards Pompeii. It was as if night had fallen in the city. The evacuation was underway, by this point, but there had already been casualties. These bodies were covered with a shell of pumice and decayed normally, their remains unpreserved. But it was the final stages of the eruption that left Pompeii preserved for a seeming eternity.

At 1:00 am, twelve hours after the first eruption, the volcanic cloud began to collapse and a surge of super hot gas and ash, called a pyroclastic surge, rushed towards the city and destroyed everything in its path. This first surge did not make it to the city, but coated the countryside in ash. By 7:30 am, a pyroclastic surge reached the city. Around two thousand people were left in the city by this point, people who were unable to escape, and the heat of the surge killed them instantly. It was moving at around 60 miles per hour with temperatures as high as 900 degrees. This fine, superheated ash coated the entire city, forming a porous shell around the bodies of the people and animals still in the city. Within these shells, decay took its usual path, but the tissue left impressions in the hardened ash. Within hollow forms, only bones and jewelry remained.

Excavation of Pompeii began in 1748, and at first, there was no way to preserve the forms. At the time, archaeological exploration was little more than treasure hunting. But by the early nineteenth century, the field had become more scholarly, and one archaeologist came up with the idea of carefully filling the hollow forms with plaster to preserve the body shape. Today, casts are made either with plaster or clear resin that allows the physical remains to be seen within the cast.

Today, Pompeii's unique view into the past is at risk. Only about 100 casts have been made of the remains. Early archaeological efforts damaged the city, and even today's archaeologists must sometimes cause damage while they excavate. These modern archaeologists document their digs carefully, and purposefully have left large areas covered so that they will be preserved for future generations. Pollution, weather, and tourism also cause damage to the area. Today's caregivers are working hard to control these conditions so we can continue to learn from Pompeii.

Roman fresco from the Villa dei Misteri. Photo by gisleh.

Graffiti

Today, we communicate with countless numbers of people by writing on a virtual "wall" through social media websites. In ancient times, the inhabitants of Pompeii and Herculaneum communicated by literally writing on a wall. There are thousands of examples of preserved graffiti, and many of them will sound familiar today, whether it calls to mind a Facebook post or graffiti in a modern bathroom stall. One wall bore so much graffiti that someone with a sense of humor added the following inscription:

"O walls, you have held up so much tedious graffiti that I am amazed that you have not already collapsed in ruin."

While historic art often gives us a polished, perfect, beautiful representation of a culture; graffiti is a spontaneous snapshot of a moment in the past. These inscriptions didn't have a lot of premeditation in them and they weren't meant to be lasting monuments. That may be why they seem so charming and relatable to our own daily life.

A note to educators: if your student is interested in researching more about Pompeii's graffiti we highly advise reviewing all content for age appropriateness.

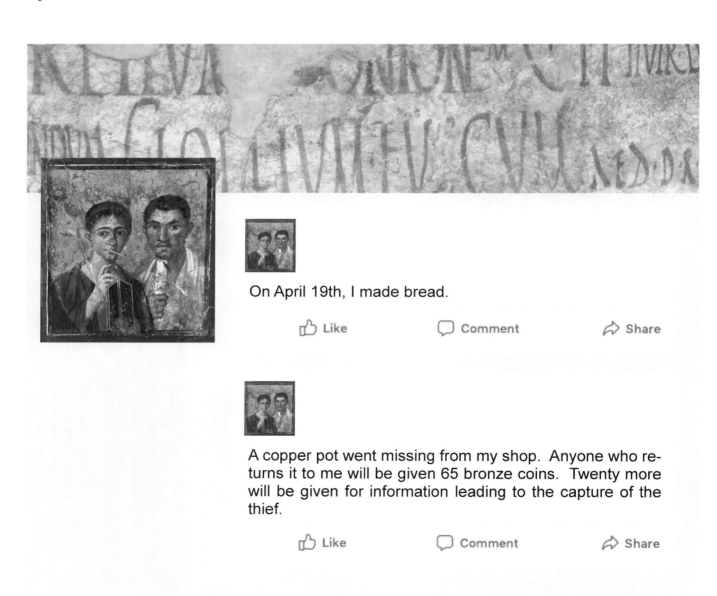

On April 19th, I made bread.

👍 Like　　　💬 Comment　　　➤ Share

A copper pot went missing from my shop. Anyone who returns it to me will be given 65 bronze coins. Twenty more will be given for information leading to the capture of the thief.

👍 Like　　　💬 Comment　　　➤ Share

FURTHER READING

All Ages

Escape from Pompeii by Christina Balit. Readers of all ages will be drawn in by the exciting story of two young people escaping the destructive force of Vesuvius. Please pre-read for sensitive learners.

The Secrets of Vesuvius by Sara C. Bisel. The author, a physical anthropologist, weaves together her own analysis of the remains of the people of Herculaneum (the city on the other side of Vesuvius) with a narrative based on her discoveries. Learners of all ages will enjoy the fictionalized account, while those with an interest in anthropology will love reading a first-hand account of discovery. This book is out of print but widely available.

Bodies from the Ash: Life and Death in Ancient Pompeii by James M. Deem. I recommend this book for readers of all ages because it provides a very clear timeline of the events surrounding the eruption. However, educators should preview this book for sensitive children as there are many images of the plaster casts which they may find disturbing.

Ages 5-9

Pompeii...Buried Alive! by Edith Kunhardt. This is a Level 4 Step into Reading book suitable as a read-aloud for new readers or as independent reading for those reading on a second or third grade reading level. It describes both the eruption and the archaeology.

Pompeii: Lost and Found by Mary Pope Osborne. You might recognize the author from her famous **Magic Treehouse** series, but this is a picture book that describes the events of the eruption, life in Pompeii, and the archaeological discovery in an easy-to-read narrative with beautiful illustrations. I especially like the illustrations for more sensitive learners who might be upset by photographic images of the plaster casts made of the people of Pompeii.

Ages 10-15

I Survived the Destruction of Pompeii by Lauren Tarshis. This is part of a series of stories about young people surviving major disasters. It not only describes what it felt like to be present for the eruption of Vesuvius, but gives a peek into the life of a Roman slave during the 1st century.

Pompeii by Peter Connolly. For those interested in what life was like in Pompeii, look no further than this book with its rich details about rooms, businesses, people, the disaster, and more. Connolly provides diagrams of the city, photographs of the city today, and pictures of the artifacts that help tell Pompeii's story.

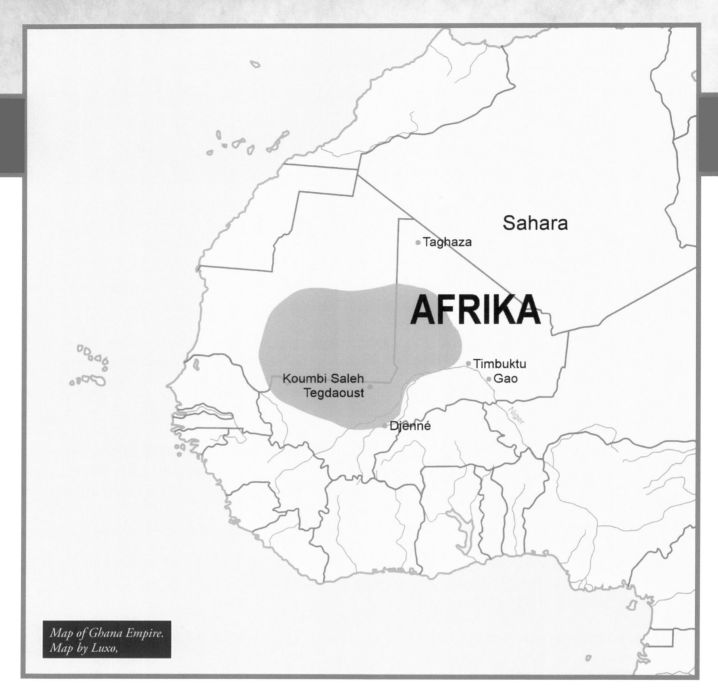

The capital of the Ghana Empire, Kumbi or Koumbi Saleh, was a center of a trading system that stretched from sub-Saharan Africa to the Mediterranean. The Soninke people, who called their own land Wagadu, acted as intermediaries. They brought goods up from the south and sent them north across the Sahara with the nomadic Berbers, who rode camels across the desert and provided access to Mediterranean markets. This access meant trade with Europe, which sent horses, cloth, swords, and books across the desert in exchange for the riches of Wagadu. Gold, kola nuts, ivory, salt, and slaves all came through Kumbi, protected by armed guards that worked for the king to ensure the safety of merchant traders and their goods. The empire began during the 4th century, rising in prominence until its height from around 800 AD/CE to 1100 AD/CE. In 1240 AD/CE, the rising Empire of Mali annexed the fading empire of Ghana, becoming the next great West African Kingdom.

The Ghana Empire was located in present day Mauritania, Mali, and Senegal, about 400 miles northwest of modern Ghana. It is possible that modern Ghana took its name from this ancient empire upon

GHANA EMPIRE

gaining independence, but the true origins of the modern country's name are still debated. We do, however, know a great deal about the ancient Empire's history. Much of our knowledge comes from Arab scholars such as the astronomer Al Fazari who called it "the land of gold" and called its king the "richest in the world." During this time, Arab scholars traveled in great numbers to West Africa, drawn by trade and positions of influence with the king. The kings of Ghana maintained their African religious beliefs, but these scholars increased their influence over the next several hundred years.

The long reign of the Ghana Empire began in ancient times and ended in the period known as the High Middle Ages. In Europe, this period used to be known as "The Dark Ages" in reference to the decline in literature and cultural achievements after the fall of the Roman Empire. While Latin literature did decline in this period, the term Dark Ages has fallen out of favor with most historians. During this time, Christianity had become the dominant religion in Europe and began to move towards its modern shape as nations like Scotland solidified into single kingdoms.

Whether or not one thinks of this time as a dark intellectual age in Europe, this was not the case globally. In West Africa and the Middle East, Islamic scholarship thrived and great advances occurred during this period, including great advances in the field of algebra. The first hospital was founded in modern-day Iraq in the 10th century. Chinese culture also flourished, with this period considered the very height of classical Chinese civilization. The Chinese invented the first movable type in the eleventh century. It would take more than 400 years before Europeans caught up, when Gutenberg came onto the scene. In a more explosive area, the Chinese first discovered gunpowder (9th century) and then invented fireworks a hundred years later.

In the Americas, things were just as busy. The Toltecs and the Mixtecs thrived in Central America, and the Mississippian Culture flourished in North America, with trade networks spanning most of the North American continent. Other American empires rose and fell during this period, most notably the Wari culture of western South America.

This ancient baobab tree in the Réserve de Bandia, Sénégal, forms a living mausoleum for the remains of famed local griots. Photo by Ji-Elle.

Storytelling

In ancient Ghana, storytelling was an important tradition, and the griots, or storytellers, played a pivotal role in society. They were considered wise and treated with high respect, not only on the topic of stories but also for historic knowledge and political counsel as well. As a part of their apprenticeship in the trade (usually passed down in a family), a griot had to memorize complex genealogies, historical events, and, of course, stories and songs. Because they had such an extensive knowledge of history and the relationships of the people around them, they were able to offer wise advice to the leaders and kings who hired them. This knowledge also made the griot an extremely valuable member of the village's society. While anyone could tell stories, each village had only one official griot, and trying to steal another village's griot could start a war. The griot had no other job besides learning and sharing his knowledge. In the evenings, when the village's inhabitants were done with the day's work, he might beat a drum or shake a rattle as he called out the words "Come hear! Come hear!" Adults and children alike would come to his call, ready to hear stories of gods and goddesses, warfare and battles, or great heroes or kings.

Senegalese Wolof griot, 1890

Griots began as court musicians, providing entertainment at celebrations such as weddings, naming ceremonies, and religious rituals. While male griots gained more prestige as advisors and messengers, female storytellers called griottes continued to fulfill this earlier traditional role. They sang at weddings and to women on their wedding nights. They also sang of the relationships between men and women. While griots used spoken as well as sung words, the griottes primarily practiced their art through song.

The art of storytelling is still practiced in modern times and one of the most enduring and loved characters to come out of ancient Ghana and into the modern era is Anansi the Spider. Perhaps the reason he has been loved and laughed over for so long is that he isn't really a hero: he is charming, but also tricky, selfish, and lazy. He'll scheme for a day to avoid an hour's work, and often his deceptions backfire.

Educator's Note: In our story, we use the word griot for storyteller. We used this word because more modern readers may be familiar with the word. The Sodinke people would more likely have used the word jeli.

Textiles

The creation of a piece of cloth in the Ghana Empire begins in a cotton field. The farmer plants rows of seeds and waits patiently for two to three months for the plant to sprout and burst into blossom. The flowers then wilt and die, leaving behind a pod called a cotton boll. This pod starts green, but begins to stretch and turn brown as the fibers inside grow in the warmth of the sun. At last, the pod bursts open, the fluffy white fibers popping out. Then the pods are harvested by hand. Each fluffy ball must be picked clean of seeds before it can be combed and spun into cotton thread.

Women and young girls are responsible for the spinning and dyeing of the fluffy white fibers. Spinning wheels are unknown here, and they use a drop spindle. A drop spindle looks somewhat like a toy top. For coloring, they use dyes made from plants to turn the white thread to yellow, brown, green, red, or blue. Then the thread is ready for the weavers. The weaver might use a double heddle loom to weave narrow strips of fabric or a single heddle loom to weave a wider strip of fabric. This weaver, probably a man, will then give the narrow strips to someone else to be sewn together into a larger piece of fabric that can be cut into clothing.

Photo by JonRichfield

Anansi the Spider

Many cultures have stories of a trickster god or spirit. Anansi the Spider was the trickster of the Akan people of modern-day Ghana. According to Akan oral tradition, their people originally came from the Ghana Empire. The people of West Africa took their Anansi stories with them across the Atlantic when the people were captured and sold as slaves in the Americas. The stories grew and changed in the Caribbean, and became part of Afro-Caribbean culture. Back in Ghana, Anansi stories remained an important part of oral tradition. Today the stories of Anansi's adventures have found audiences worldwide. This is the story of how Anansi became the god of all stories.

Children, I do not say that this story is true. Take this story and then let it go. Once there were no stories in the world. Nyame, the Sky God, had all of the stories for his own. Anansi the Spider wanted the stories to share with other people, so he built a web, up up and up into the sky to buy the stories from Nyame. When Anansi told Nyame that he wanted to buy the stories, Nyame laughed and laughed and laughed.

"Little Spider, you cannot afford to buy my stories," Nyame said. "You must bring me Onini the Python, Osebo the Leopard, the Mboro Hornets, and Mmoatia the Fairy, who no one ever sees. Bring me these things and I will sell you all of my stories." Anansi nodded and climbed back down his web. While he had pretended bravery in front of Nyame, Anansi had no idea how to capture these fearsome creatures. He asked his wife for help, and together they came up with a plan to capture Onini the Python.

The next day, Anansi went into the jungle. He carried a large stick and waved it into the air, muttering loudly.

"No, no, no. She cannot be right. There is no way this stick is longer." Without warning, Onini unfurled from a tree branch and hissed irritably at Anansi.

"Ananssssssi, you have disssturbed my sssslumber. What issss the matter?"

"Oh, great Onini. My wife and I cannot agree. She says that you are no longer than this stick, and I know that you are longer than the stick." The snake slithered to the ground.

"Little sssspider, lay down your sssssstick and we shall ssssseee ssssooon enough." Anansi did as he was told and the snake stretched out along the stick. The snake's body kept coiling as Anansi tugged and pulled, refusing to lie still against the stick.

"No, no, it isn't working," Anansi declared. "You aren't quite straight so you are not quite at your full length." Onini tried again, but Anansi had an idea. "Let me help you. I will use my silk to tie you to the stick and make you straight. Then we will prove to my wife just how big and mighty you truly are." The proud snake agreed, and was soon bound tightly to to the stick with spider silk. Anansi gleefully took the hissing and furious snake up to Nyame.

"You have succeeded in one task, Anansi. But you must bring me more to pay my price." Anansi scuttled back down his silken thread to his web, and asked his wife to help him come up with another plan.

The next day, while Osebo the Leopard slept, Anansi got to work. He dug a deep pit, right in the middle of the path Osebo took to the watering hole each night. It was hard work, but he finished as the sun was setting and quickly covered the hole with branches. He hid behind a tree and waited. Soon enough, he heard a crash and ran to the trap. Osebo the Leopard paced, snarling, at the bottom of the hole. When the leopard saw Anansi peering down, he growled up at the spider.

"I have fallen into this trap. You must help me get out." Anansi backed away from the edge, pretending to be afraid.

"Oh no, Great Leopard. If I get you out, you will eat me!" Osebo's tone changed to a purr.

"Anansi, I promise not to eat you if you help me out of this trap." Anansi agreed, and began releasing silk threads down into the hole. As the leopard tried to climb the spider's silk, it twisted around his legs. The more he struggled, the more he became entangled. By the time Anansi pulled the leopard out of the hole, only the big cat's fierce eyes could be seen, glaring at the spider. Anansi dragged his prize up to Nyame and deposited Osebo at the sky god's feet.

"Well, little spider, you have now brought me two of the things I have asked for. We shall see if you are able to bring me the rest of my price." Anansi bowed and scurried back home to his wife. His clever wife helped him come up with a plan to capture the Mboro Hornets.

The next day, Anansi walked through the jungle, carrying a calabash[1] filled with water. When he heard the fierce buzzing of the hornets' nest, he quickly cut a leaf from a plantain tree. Then, standing next to the nest, he dumped half of the water on himself and the rest onto the nest. When the angry hornets came swarming out of the nest, he spoke to them in a pitying voice.

"Oh, you poor hornets! The rains have come early this year. Quick, fly into my calabash, and I will keep you dry." The grateful hornets made a beeline for safety, flying into the gourd. As soon as the last one was inside, Anansi covered the hole with the plantain leaf and secured it with his silk. He carried the angrily buzzing bundle up to Nyame. The sky god tried to cover his surprise that Anansi had been so successful.

"You have done well, Anansi. But you still must bring me that evil-tempered fairy, Mmoatia." As the spider left, Nyame felt sure that the little spider would not succeed in this last endeavor for the fairy was invisible. Anansi, however, consulted with his clever wife and they came up with one more plan. She pounded yams into a paste, the favorite food of the fairies while Anansi carved a doll out of wood and covered it with sticky resin from a gum tree. The next day, Anansi took it the yams and the doll to a place deep in the jungle where the fairies lived. He set up the doll with the bowl of yams in its lap, and spun silk so thin it was nearly invisible. He tied one end of the thread to the doll's head. Then, holding the other end, he hid himself behind a tree. Soon, he heard a little voice but saw no one. The voice spoke to the doll.

"Oh, Little One, may I have some of your yams?" Anansi pulled on the thread, making the doll nod its head. The bowl of yams floated up, and bit by bit, the yams disappeared into thin air. When the bowl was empty, it dropped to the ground with a clatter. The voice spoke again. "Thank you, that was delicious." Anansi, and the doll, remained motionless. The voice spoke again, this time sounded irritated.

"Did you hear me? I said thank you! Answer me, or I will have to hit you!" When the doll did not answer, it was suddenly struck by an invisible force and its head wobbled. "Let go of me," the voice shrieked. "Or I will hit you again!" Almost immediately, the head wobbled a second time. Now the voice was really howling. "Let me go, or I will kick you!" Again, the doll shook as it was struck. Soon, it was rolling around on the ground as the voice screamed and shouted. Anansi came out of hiding and quickly wrapped his silk around the doll and the invisible fairy. His work complete, he carried the fairy, still tied to the doll, up to Nyame.

Nyame looked at the spider and the protesting bundle. "Well, Anansi, you have brought me everything I asked for. The stories are now yours. Let it be known that you paid the price. From this day, they shall be known as spider stories."

<table>
<tr><td>

FURTHER READING

All Ages
Daily Life in Ancient and Modern Timbuktu by Larry Brook. I recommend this book as a way of connecting the Ghana Empire to the Africa of today, and providing information about everything that came in between. Out of print but widely available used.

Ages 5-9
Sub-Saharan Africa by Lisa Zamosky. The book is an overall history of the region, but has sections on Kush, Aksum, and Ghana.

Ages 10-15
The Royal Kingdoms of Ghana, Mali, and Songhay: Life in Medieval Africa by Patricia and Frederick McKissack. This longer volume provides a more in depth look into the progressions of these kingdoms, including great detail about the Ghana Empire. There is also a great timeline putting events in West Africa into a context of world history as a whole.

</td></tr>
</table>

1.   A type of gourd

Conclusion

We leave our story with Ghana, and not the Fall of Rome, because Ghana is such an excellent example of a culture that straddles the time divide between ancient and medieval history. The time definition of the Middle Ages, once called the Dark Ages, is purely defined by western European history. The Fall of Rome had an enormous impact on western civilization, but other civilizations around the world also rose and fell. Historians have traditionally used the term ancient history in a somewhat willy-nilly way. For European history, it's everything from the invention of writing in the Middle East to the Fall of Rome. For Asian history, that works pretty well too. And yet, because we define history as something that has been written down, that left large swathes of Africa, the Americas, and of course, Australia, as "prehistoric" until European arrival. Even now, writers who describe the "ancient history" of the Americas includes the Maya. Like Ghana, they straddle the timeline between ancient and medieval history and were contemporaries of Charlemagne and the writer of Beowulf. We will be looking at their classical period when we get to the Middle Ages. The Incans and Aztecs were at the height of their civilizations well into the medieval era.

But wait! You might be thinking. We didn't talk about the Persians or the Spartans or Stonehenge! You're right. You could spend a lifetime learning about all the fascinating people, places and events of the past. We've chosen to visit places that are often overlooked but relevant in our global world. There are many fabulous historical resources that cover other periods in great detail. Check out our general reading list to continue your ancient history studies.

Timbuktu seen from a distance by Heinrich Barth

GENERAL HISTORY RECOMMENDED READING

All Ages
Motel of Mysteries by David Macaulay. Unlike other books on our reading lists, this book is actually not about ancient history at all. It is a fictionalized account of an archaeological expedition of the ancient country of Usa...in the year 4022. I recommend this book to start an ancient history study because it shows the limitations of archaeology, especially when we don't have translated writing.

The Kingfisher Book of the Ancient World From the Ice Age to the Fall of Rome by Hazel Mary Martell. This book is included because it has sections on some of the cultures with limited book lists. It can also provide a jumping off point for continuing ancient history studies by sparking interests in the civilizations we did not cover.

Archaeology for Kids: Uncovering the Mysteries of Our Past by RIchard Panchyk. We talked a lot in this book about how archaeology helps us understand the past. This book alternates description with hands on for kids who get excited about archaeology. It pairs well with *Motel of Mysteries*.

Ages 10-15
Outrageous Women of Ancient Times by Vicki León. This book has limited availability, but is worth it if you can find it. The biographies of women from the ancient world had me laughing and admiring at the same time.

Index

Locators in "**bold**" are
for pictures/figures.

CPSIA information can be obtained
at www.ICGtesting.com
Printed in the USA
BVHW050053310122
627600BV00008B/424